BLACK&DECKER®

PORTABLE

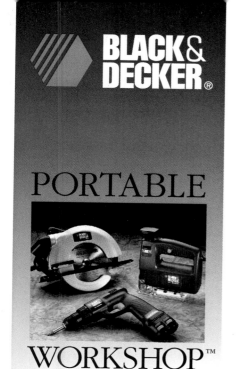

WORKSHOP™

Basic Wood Projects
with Portable Power Tools

W9-CQF-941

Maximizing Minimal Space

For Betty

all the best for 2000!

♡ Elyse

Copyright © 1996 Cy DeCosse Incorporated
5900 Green Oak Drive, Minnetonka, Minnesota 55343
1-800-328-3895 All rights reserved
Printed in U.S.A.

Credits

Group Executive Editor: Paul Currie
Project Director: Mark Johanson
Associate Creative Director: Tim Himsel
Managing Editor: Kristen Olson
Project Manager: Lori Holmberg
Lead Project Designer: Jim Huntley
Editors: Mark Biscan, Steve Meyer
Editor & Technical Artist: Jon Simpson
Editorial Assistant: Andrew Sweet
Lead Art Director: Gina Seeling
Technical Production Editor: Greg Pluth
Project Designer: Steve Meyer
Contributing Draftsman: John T. Drigot

*Vice President of Photography
  & Production:* Jim Bindas
Copy Editor: Janice Cauley
Shop Supervisor: Phil Juntti
Lead Builder: John Nadeau
Builders: Troy Johnson, Rob Johnstone
Production Staff: Laura Hokkanen, Tom
  Hoops, Jeanette Moss, Gary Sandin,
  Mike Schauer, Brent Thomas,
  Greg Wallace, Kay Wethern

Creative Photo Coordinator:
  Cathleen Shannon
Studio Manager: Marcia Chambers
Lead Photographer: Rebecca Schmitt
Photographer: Steve Smith
Photography Assistants: Dan Cary,
  Herb Schnabel
Production Manager: Stasia Dorn
Printed on American paper by:
  Inland Press 99 98 97 96 / 5 4 3 2 1

CY DeCOSSE INCORPORATED

OWLES
Enthusiast Media

Chairman/CEO: Philip L. Penny
Chairman Emeritus: Cy DeCosse
President/COO: Nino Tarantino
Executive V.P./Editor-in-Chief:
  William B. Jones

Created by: The editors of Cy DeCosse
  Incorporated, in cooperation with Black
  & Decker. ● **BLACK&DECKER** is a trademark
  of the Black & Decker Corporation and
  is used under license.

Library of Congress
Cataloging-in-Publication Data

Maximizing minimal space.
       p. cm.—(Portable workshop)
  At head of title: Black & Decker.
  ISBN   0-86573-670-7 (hardcover).

1. Furniture making--Amateurs' manuals. 2. Built-in
furniture--Amateurs' manuals.
I. Cy DeCosse Incorporated.
II. Black & Decker Corporation (Towson, MD)
III. Series.
TT195.M367 1996
684.1--dc20   96-18878

Contents

Introduction

Home furnishings, like cars, are becoming more space and size conscious with every passing year. Also like cars, they are becoming more expensive. But where cars are built for you by workers in Detroit or Japan, you can build your own home furnishings in your basement or garage. In *Maximizing Minimal Space*, the Black & Decker® *Portable Workshop™* brings you 20 simple, clever building projects that conquer the space issue—and without sacrificing style or ease of construction.

All the projects in this book can be built with tools you probably already own, and with techniques you probably already know. You don't need to be an experienced woodworker to make them. A tile-top coffee table with a spacious storage shelf; a Country-style armoire that converts a few feet of floor space into a freestanding closet; a slender bookcase that practically melts into the wall in a narrow hallway; whether you live in a 20-room mansion or a two-room efficiency, these hardworking building projects will help you create the space you need for all your stuff.

For each of the projects in *Maximizing Minimal Space*, you will find a complete cutting list, a materials-shopping list, a detailed construction drawing, full-color photographs of the major steps, and clear, easy-to-follow directions that guide you through every step of the project.

The Black & Decker® *Portable Workshop™* book series gives weekend do-it-yourselfers the power to build beautiful wood projects without spending a lot of money. Ask your local bookseller for more information on other volumes in this innovative new series.

NOTICE TO READERS

This book provides useful instructions, but we cannot anticipate all of your working conditions or the characteristics of your materials and tools. For safety, you should use caution, care, and good judgment when following the procedures described in this book. Consider your own skill level and the instructions and safety precautions associated with the various tools and materials shown. Neither the publisher nor Black & Decker® can assume responsibility for any damage to property, injury to persons, or losses incurred as a result of misuse of the information provided.

Organizing Your Worksite

Portable power tools and hand tools offer a level of convenience that is a great advantage over stationary power tools. But using them safely and conveniently requires some basic housekeeping. Whether you are working in a garage, a basement or outdoors, it is important that you establish a flat, dry holding area where you can store tools. Set aside a piece of plywood on sawhorses, or dedicate an area of your workbench for tool storage, and be sure to return tools to that area once you are finished with them. It is also important that all waste, including lumber scraps and sawdust, be disposed of in a timely fashion. Check with your local waste disposal department before throwing away any large scraps of building materials or any finishing-material containers.

If you are using corded power tools outdoors, always use grounded extension cords (called *GFCI* cords), connected to a grounded power source. Keep cords neat and out of traffic lanes at all times. Where practical, use cordless power tools to minimize risk from power cords.

> *Safety Tips*
> *•Always wear eye and hearing protection when operating power tools and performing any other dangerous activities.*
> *•Choose a well-ventilated work area when cutting or shaping wood and when using finishing products.*

Tools & Materials

At the start of each project, you will find a set of symbols that show which power tools are used to complete the project as it is shown (see below). You will also need a set of basic hand tools: a hammer, screwdrivers, tape measure, a level, a combination square, C-clamps, and pipe or bar clamps. You also will find a shopping list of all the construction materials you will need. Miscellaneous materials and hardware are listed with the cutting list that accompanies the construction drawing. When buying lumber, note that the "nominal" size of the lumber is usually larger than the "actual size." For example, a 2 × 4 is actually 1½ × 3½".

Power Tools You Will Use

Circular saw *to make straight cuts. For long cuts and rip-cuts, use a straight-edge guide. Install a carbide-tipped combination blade for most projects.*

Drills: *use a cordless drill for drilling pilot holes and counterbores, and to drive screws; use an electric drill for sanding and grinding tasks.*

Jig saw *for making contoured cuts and internal cuts. Use a combination wood blade for most projects where you will cut pine, cedar or plywood.*

Power sander *to prepare wood for a finish and to smooth out sharp edges. Owning several power sanders (⅓-sheet, ¼-sheet, and belt) is helpful.*

Belt sander *for resurfacing rough wood. Can also be used as a stationary sander when mounted on its side on a flat worksurface.*

Router *to cut decorative edges and roundovers in wood. As you gain more experience, use routers for cutting grooves (like dadoes) to form joints.*

Guide to Building Materials Used in This Book

•Sheet goods:

PLYWOOD: Basic sheet good sold in several grades (from CDX to AB) and thicknesses. Inexpensive to moderate.

BIRCH PLYWOOD: A highly workable, readily available alternative to pine or fir plywood. A good cabinet-making material, birch plywood has a very smooth surface that is excellent for painting or staining, and generally has fewer voids in the edges that require filling. Moderately expensive.

MELAMINE BOARD (CLAD BOARD): Particleboard with a glossy, polymerized surface that is water-resistant and easy to clean. Inexpensive.

•Dimension lumber:

PINE: A basic softwood used for many interior projects. "Select" and "#2 or better" are suitable grades. Relatively inexpensive.

RED OAK: A common hardwood that stains well and is very durable. Relatively inexpensive.

ASPEN: A soft, easily worked hardwood. Commonly available at building centers. Must be sealed to get an even stain. Usually sold in standard dimensions and in extra-wide glued panels. Good for painting. Moderate.

Guide to Fasteners & Adhesives Used in This Book

•Fasteners & hardware:

WOOD SCREWS: Brass or steel; most projects use screws with a #6 or #8 shank. Can be driven with a power driver.

NAILS & BRADS: Finish nails can be set below the wood surface: common (box) nails have wide, flat heads; brads or wire nails are very small, thin fasteners with small heads.

Misc.: Door pulls & knobs; butt hinges, strap hinges; corner braces; swivel casters; plastic or nylon glides; magnetic door catches; roller catches; other specialty hardware as indicated.

•Adhesives:

WOOD GLUE: Yellow glue is suitable for all projects in this book.

MOISTURE-RESISTANT WOOD GLUE: Any exterior wood glue, such as plastic resin glue.

TILE ADHESIVE: An adhesive specially designed for ceramic tile.

•Miscellaneous materials:

Wood plugs (for filling counterbores); ceramic tile; dowel rods.

Finishing Your Project

Before applying finishing materials like stain or paint, fill all nail holes and blemishes with wood putty or filler. Also, fill all voids in any exposed plywood edges with wood putty. Sand the dried putty smooth. Alternative: fill counterbored pilot holes with wood plugs if applying stain. Sand wood surfaces with medium-grit sandpaper (100- to 150-grit), then finish-sand with fine sandpaper (180- to 220-grit). Wipe the surfaces clean, then apply at least two coats of paint (enamel paint is most durable), or apply stain and at least two coats of topcoating product (water-based polyurethane is a good choice).

Card Table

This stylish table proves that card tables don't always have to be flimsy and unappealing.

CONSTRUCTION MATERIALS

Quantity	Lumber
1	½" × 4 × 4' oak plywood
2	2 × 2" × 8' pine
2	1 × 3" × 8' pine
3	¾ × ¾" × 8' oak edge molding

The card table has always been thought of as overflow seating for those houseguests who are most lacking in seniority. But the diners assigned to this contemporary wood card table will feel more like they have favored status. The warm tones of the oak tabletop contrast vividly with the painted legs and apron for a lovely effect that will blend into just about any setting—from formal dining to a Friday night poker game.

The fold-up legs on this card table are attached with special fasteners designed just for card tables. You can find these fasteners, as well as the oak apron trim, at most hardware stores or woodworker's shops.

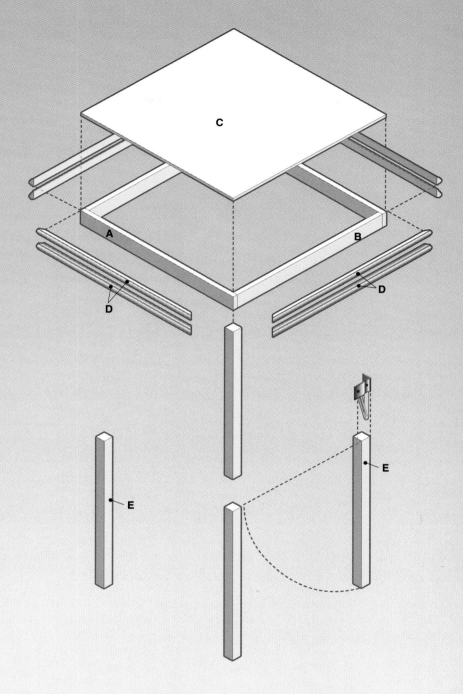

OVERALL SIZE:
29" HIGH
33¼" WIDE
33¼" DEEP

Cutting List				
Key	**Part**	**Dimension**	**Pcs.**	**Material**
A	Side apron	¾ × 2½ × 32"	2	Pine
B	End apron	¾ × 2½ × 30½"	2	Pine
C	Tabletop	½ × 32 × 32"	1	Oak plywood

Cutting List				
Key	**Part**	**Dimension**	**Pcs.**	**Material**
D	Edge trim	¾ × ¾ × 32"	8	Oak molding
E	Leg	1½ × 1½ × 28"	4	Pine

Materials: Wood glue, #6 × 1½" wood screws, 2" machine bolts with locking nuts (4), 3d finish nails, oak-tinted wood putty, card-table leg fasteners (4), finishing materials.

Note: Measurements reflect the actual thickness of dimensional lumber.

Directions: Card Table

BUILD THE TABLETOP. The tabletop for this card table is a sheet of oak plywood framed with an apron made from 1 × 3 pine. Strips of oak molding are attached around the top and bottom of the apron to protect the edges of the apron when the table is being stored, and to add a nice decorative accent. Start by cutting the side aprons (A) and end aprons (B) to length. Fasten the end aprons between the side aprons with glue and countersunk wood screws to form a square frame **(photo A).** Keep the outside edges and surfaces of the aprons flush. Next, cut the tabletop (C) to size from ½"-thick plywood using a circular saw and straightedge cutting guide. Position the plywood tabletop on the frame, keeping the outside edges of the table-top flush with the outer surfaces of the aprons. Fasten the tabletop to the top of the frame with glue and 3d finish nails **(photo B).**

SHAPE THE LEGS. Cut the legs (E) to length. Lay out ¾"-radius curves on each leg end using a compass, and cut the curves with a jig saw to form the roundovers. These allow the legs to pivot smoothly inside the card-table leg fasteners.

TIP

Use sanding sealer before you apply wood stain to create more even absorption that helps elimi-nate blotchy finishes. Sanding sealer is a clear product, usually applied with a brush. Check the backs of the product labels on all the finishing products you plan to apply to make sure they are compatible. To be safe, choose either water-based or oil-based products for the whole project.

Fasten the end aprons between the side aprons with glue and coun-tersunk wood screws to construct the apron frame.

PAINT THE FRAME & LEGS. If you plan to apply a combina-tion finish, as we did, you'll find it easier and neater to paint the legs and frame before you assemble the table and at-tach the apron trim. Sand the pine surfaces to be painted with medium-grit sandpaper. Wipe the surfaces clean, then apply primer to the aprons and legs. Apply several coats of enamel paint in the color of your choice (we chose blue).

ATTACH THE EDGE TRIM. When the paint has dried, at-tach the edge trim to the table-top edges and the aprons. We used plain oak shelf-edge molding, but you may wish to use a more decorative molding type (but be sure to use oak to match the tabletop). Start by cutting the edge trim pieces (D) to length. You'll need to cut a 45° miter at each end of each trim piece, using a power miter saw or hand miter box. The best method is to cut a miter on one end of the first

piece, and position the trim against the apron or tabletop edges. Mark the appropriate length on the uncut end of the trim, cut the 45° miter, and then fasten the edge trim to the aprons or the tabletop edge us-ing wood glue and 3d finish nails. Drill pilot holes through the trim pieces before driving the nails—because it is so hard, oak is prone to splitting. Continue this process, keeping the mitered ends tight when marking for length, until all edge trim has been attached to the aprons and tabletop edges **(photo C).** Be sure to keep the tops of the upper trim pieces flush with the surface of the tabletop. Keep the bottoms of the lower trim pieces flush with the bottoms of the aprons.

FASTEN THE LEGS & HARD-WARE. The legs are attached to the table with locking card-table leg fasteners. First, attach a card-table leg fastener to the

Fasten the oak plywood tabletop to the top of the apron frame with glue and finish nails. Oak trim is used to cover the plywood edges.

The oak trim fastened at the top and bottom of the apron provides protection and a decorative accent.

Attach the card-table leg fasteners to the rounded ends of the legs, then attach them at the inside corners of the tabletop frame.

rounded end of each leg by drilling a ¼"-dia. hole through the leg, then securing the fastener to the leg with a 2" machine bolt and locking nut (the fastening method may vary, depending on the brand of hardware you purchase; be sure to read any manufacturer's directions that come with the hardware). Attach the fasteners to the legs with the screws provided with the hardware. Do not tighten the screws completely yet. Next, lay the tabletop upside down on a flat worksurface. Attach the leg fasteners to the insides of the apron at each corner of the tabletop frame **(photo D).** Test the legs to make sure they fit properly when folded up, and that the fasteners operate smoothly. Also check to make sure the table is level and stable when resting on a flat surface. Make any needed adjustments to the positioning or length of the legs, then fully tighten all screws.

APPLY FINISHING TOUCHES. Set all finish-nail heads in the table surface, and cover the heads with oak-tinted wood putty. Sand the putty smooth, then sand the unfinished surfaces with medium sandpaper. Finish-sand with fine sandpaper. Wipe the surfaces, then apply sanding sealer for an even finish. Apply wood stain to color the wood (if you are using medium to dark stain, mask the painted surfaces first). Apply two or three light coats of water-based polyurethane to the entire table.

Hallway Bookcase

*A stable base that tapers to a low-profile top lets you add storage
and display space in even the tightest quarters.*

CONSTRUCTION MATERIALS

Quantity	Lumber
2	1 × 10" × 8' pine
1	1 × 8" × 6' pine
1	1 × 6" × 6' pine
3	1 × 4" × 8' pine

Hallways are frequently underutilized areas of a home. The reason is simple—large furnishings cramp the area. When foot traffic is heavy but space is at a premium, this hallway bookcase makes the most of the situation. Fitting flush against the wall, it allows you to store your books and display your knick-knacks without cluttering up the hall or consuming valuable floor space. The bookcase is tapered, so it is thinner at the top than at the bottom. This design reduces the chance of tipping and cuts down on space consumption. A very simple and inexpensive project to build, this bookcase can truly create something from nothing.

OVERALL SIZE:
60" HIGH
36" WIDE
9" DEEP

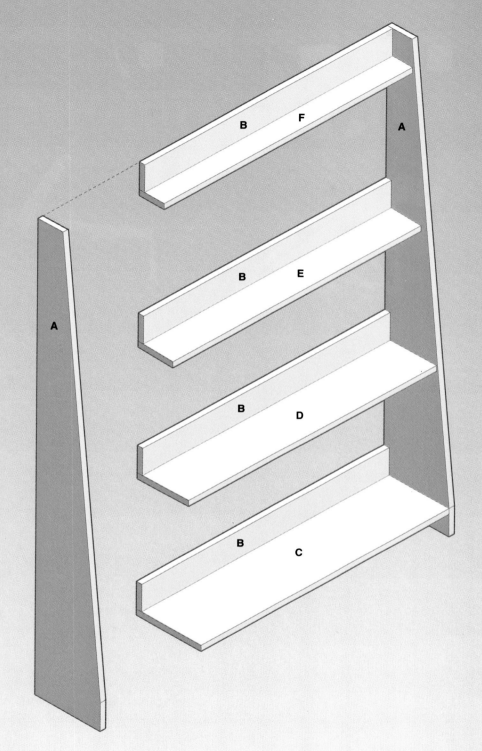

Cutting List				
Key	**Part**	**Dimension**	**Pcs.**	**Material**
A	Standard	¾ × 9¼ × 60"	2	Pine
B	Spreader	¾ × 3½ × 34½"	4	Pine
C	Shelf	¾ × 9¼ × 34½"	1	Pine

Cutting List				
Key	**Part**	**Dimension**	**Pcs.**	**Material**
D	Shelf	¾ × 7¼ × 34½"	1	Pine
E	Shelf	¾ × 5¼ × 34½"	1	Pine
F	Shelf	¾ × 3½ × 34½"	1	Pine

Materials: Wood glue, #8 × 2" wood screws, finishing materials.

Note: Measurements reflect the actual size of dimensional lumber.

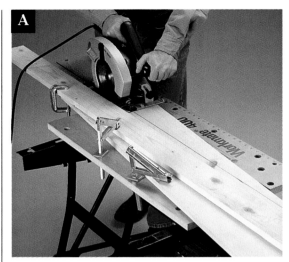

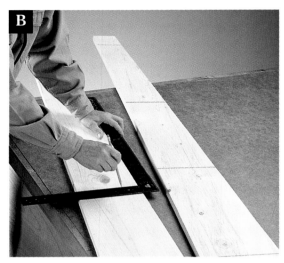

Clamp a straightedge to the standard, and make the taper cut with a circular saw.

Use a framing square to mark reference lines on the standards for shelf placement.

Directions:
Hall Bookcase

MAKE THE STANDARDS. The tapered standards are wide at the bottom for stability and narrow at the top to conserve space in a busy hallway. Start by cutting the standards (A) to length from 1 × 10 pine boards. Position the boards against each other on your worksurface to make sure they are the same length. On one standard, designate a long edge to be the front. Mark a point on the front edge of the standard, 3½" up from the bottom. Mark another point on the top of the standard, 3½" in from the back edge. Draw a straight line connecting these points to form a tapered cutting line for the standard. Clamp a straightedge to the board, parallel to the cutting line, and cut the taper with a circular saw **(photo A).** Sand the parts to smooth out any sharp edges or rough surfaces. Use the finished standard as a template to mark the tapered cutting line on the other standard, then cut and sand it to match the first.

CUT THE SHELVES & SPREAD-ERS. The shelves and spreaders are all the same length, but the shelves at the top of the hall bookcase are more narrow than those at the bottom to conform with the taper in the standards. To make sure the boards are the same length when cut, cut one spreader (B) to length, and use it as a marking guide for marking the length on the remaining spreaders and shelves (C, D, E, F). Cut the shelves and spreaders. Check the lengths again, and sand the parts to smooth out any rough edges.

MARK THE SHELF POSITIONS. Position the standards face-down on your worksurface.

Butt the back edges of the standards together. Make sure the tops and bottoms of the standards are flush. Use a framing square and a pencil to mark reference lines on each standard, 3½", 20¾", 37½" and 56½" up from the bottoms **(photo B).** These reference lines mark the tops of the shelves. Make sure the shelf reference lines are the same distance from the bottom on both standards, or you may end up with sloping shelves.

INSTALL THE SPREADERS. The spreaders help support the shelves while providing side-to-side strength for the bookcase. The spreaders also keep books and decorative objects from contacting the wall behind the bookshelf or falling back behind the shelves and out of reach. Each spreader should fit flush with the back edges of the standards, directly above each shelf reference line. Set the standards on their back edges so their outside faces are 36" apart. Position a spreader just above the bottom shelf reference lines. Drill pilot holes through the standards and into

TIP

Special tapered drill bits make drilling counterbores for screws a snap. Simply select a counterbore bit that matches the shank size of the screws you will use (usually #6 or #8), then drill a pilot hole for each screw with a plain twist bit. Counterbore the pilot holes, using the counterbore bit, to the correct depth for the wood plugs that will be inserted into the counterbores.

The spreaders fit between the bookcase standards. Make sure the bookcase is square as you fasten them in place.

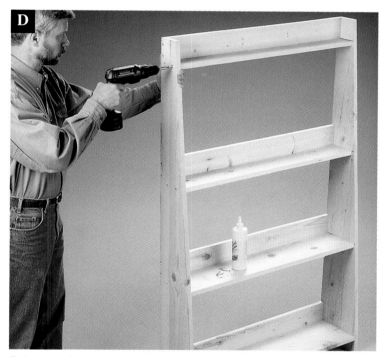

Drive wood screws through the pilot holes in the standards and into the ends of the shelves.

TIP

Anchor smaller furnishings to the wall in heavy traffic areas. In many cases, as with this open-back hallway bookcase, the exposed spreaders can be used as strips for screwing the project to the wall. For best results, drive screws into wall studs through the top spreader and at least one lower spreader. Counterbore the screws, cover the heads with wood plugs, then paint the plugs to match.

INSTALL THE SHELVES. Position the bottom shelf between the standards. Make sure the top edge of the bottom shelf is butted up against the bottom edge of the bottom spreader and is flush with the reference line. Drill pilot holes through the standards and into the ends of the shelf, and through the shelf and into the bottom edge of the spreader. (Because the screw holes underneath the shelf will not be visible, you don't need to counterbore and plug them. Countersink them slightly so you can apply wood putty before finishing.) Apply glue to the ends of the shelf and the bottom edge of the spreader, and attach the shelf with #8 × 2" wood screws. Attach the remaining shelves in the same way, working your way up **(photo D).**

APPLY FINISHING TOUCHES. Insert glued, ⅜"-dia. wood plugs into all counterbored screw holes. Fill the holes underneath the shelves with wood putty, and sand all the surfaces to smooth out any rough spots. Finish-sand the entire project with fine (up to 180- or 220-grit) sandpaper. We finished the hall bookcase with a light, semitransparent wood stain and two light coats of water-based polyurethane to protect and seal the wood.

the ends of the spreader. Counterbore the pilot holes for ⅜"-dia. wood plugs. Start by attaching the bottom spreader with glue and #8 × 2" wood screws. Attach the remaining spreaders in the same way, making sure the top spreader is flush with the top edges and back edges of the standards **(photo C).** When the final

spreader has been installed, check the bookcase to make sure it is square. Measure diagonally from corner to corner. If the measurements are equal, the bookcase is square. If the project is out of square, apply pressure to one side or the other with your hand or clamps to push a it back into square before you fasten the shelves.

PROJECT
POWER TOOLS

Tile-top Coffee Table

The dramatic, contrasting textures of floor tiles and warm red oak will make you forget that this table is designed to create storage.

CONSTRUCTION MATERIALS

Quantity	Lumber
1	¾" × 4 × 8' oak plywood
2	1 × 2" × 8' oak
2	1 × 4" × 8' oak
1	⅞ × ⅞" × 8' oak corner molding
21	6 × 6" floor tiles

Functionally, the trim size and the amply proportioned storage shelf are the two most important features of this tile-top coffee table. But most people won't notice that. They'll be too busy admiring the striking tile table-top and the clean oak lines of the table base.

Measuring in at a convenient 44½" wide × 20" deep, this coffee table will fit nicely even in smaller rooms. The shelf below is ideal for storing books, magazines, newspapers, photo albums or anything else you like to keep within arm's reach when sitting on your sofa.

We used 6 × 6" slate floor tiles for our coffee table, but you can use just about any type or size of floor tile you want—just be sure to use floor tile, not wall tile, which is much thinner and can fracture easily.

After you've built this tile-top coffee table, you may like it so much that you'll want to build a tile-top end table to match.

OVERALL SIZE:
16" HIGH
44½" WIDE
20" DEEP

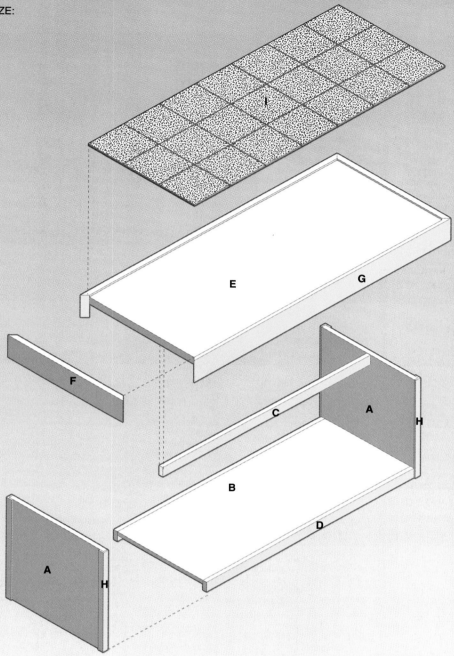

Cutting List

Key	Part	Dimension	Pcs.	Material
A	Side Panel	¾ × 16 × 15"	2	Oak Plywood
B	Shelf Panel	¾ × 14½ × 35"	1	Oak Plywood
C	Stringer	¾ × 1½ × 35"	1	Oak
D	Shelf Edge	¾ × 1½ × 35"	2	Oak
E	Top Panel	¾ × 18½ × 43"	1	Oak Plywood

Cutting List

Key	Part	Dimension	Pcs.	Material
F	End Skirt	¾ × 3½ × 20"	2	Oak
G	Side Skirt	¾ × 3½ × 44½"	2	Oak
H	Corner Trim	⅞ × ⅞ × 15"	4	Corner molding
I	Table Tiles	¼ × 18 × 42"	21	6" Ceramic Tile

Materials: Wood glue, #6 × 1½" wood screws, 3d and 6d finish nails, ⅜"-dia. oak wood plugs, ceramic tile adhesive and tinted grout, 3⁄16" plastic tile spacers, silicone grout sealer.

Specialty tools: V-notch adhesive trowel, rubber mallet, grout float.

Note: Measurements reflect the actual thickness of dimensional lumber.

Fasten the shelf edges to the shelf panel with glue and 6d finish nails.

Secure the stringer in place with glue and screws.

Directions:
Tile-top Coffee Table

ASSEMBLE THE TABLE BASE. The base for this tile-top coffee table is made up of a plywood shelf panel with oak edging that is fitted between two plywood side panels. Start by cutting the side panels (A) and shelf panel (B) to size from oak plywood using a circular saw and straightedge cutting guide. Then, cut the shelf edge (D) to length from 1 × 2 oak. Sand the edges and surfaces of the components with medium-grit sandpaper. Fasten the shelf edges to the shelf panel with glue and 6d finish nails **(photo A).** Be sure to drill pilot holes for the finish nails so you don't split the wood. Keep the top surfaces of the shelf edges and shelf panel flush when fastening. Next, set the shelf panel upright on ¾"-thick spacers. Stand a side panel upright on its bottom edge, against the end of the shelf panel, and fasten the side panel to the shelf panel with glue

Miter-cut and mount one skirt board at a time to ensure proper fit.

and 1½" wood screws driven into counterbored pilot holes. Keep the edges of the side panel flush with the outside surfaces of the shelf edging. Fasten the other side panel to the shelf panel. Cut the stringer (C) to length, and position it between the side panels, flush with the top edge and centered in the middle of the side panels. Clamp in place with a bar clamp or pipe clamp. Drill counterbored pilot holes through the side panels into the stringer. Remove the clamps and secure the stringer with glue and screws **(photo B).**

MAKE THE TABLETOP FRAME. The tabletop frame is a plywood panel framed with 1 × 4 pine. The frame extends above the plywood slightly to create a lip that covers the edges of the tile when it is installed on top of the plywood. The joints in the 1 × 4 frame are mitered— most hand-operated miter boxes can be used to cut a 1 × 4 when it's inserted on edge, but if you own a power miter box, making these cuts is an excellent time to use it. Start by cutting the top panel (E) to size from ¾"-thick oak plywood, using a circular saw and a straightedge cutting guide.

TIP

Wall tile varies greatly in size and style. This tabletop design is based on using 6 × 6" tiles with ³⁄₁₆" gaps between tiles. If you use tiles of a different size, you may need to resize the plywood table panel to fit your layout. Or, you can have the tiles cut to fit at the tile store.

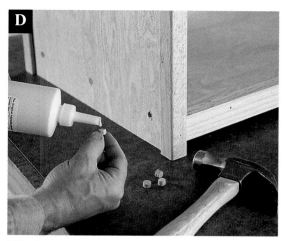

Fill all open counterbore holes with wood plugs.

Tap the tiles lightly with a rubber mallet to set them firmly in the adhesive.

Fasten the top panel to the side panels and stringer in the table base, using countersunk screws and glue. Be sure to leave an equal overhang on the ends and sides. Cut the end skirts (F) and side skirts (G) from 1 × 4 oak. Although the Cutting List on page 17 gives exact dimensions for these parts, your safest bet is to cut the first part slightly longer than the specified length, then custom-cut it to fit. Cut all the other skirt boards to length, using the first skirt board as a guide **(photo C).** Fasten the skirt boards to the edges of the top panel with glue and 6d finish nails.

FASTEN THE CORNER TRIM. Next, cut the corner trim (H) to length from oak corner molding. Fasten the corner trim to the side panel edges with glue and 3d finish nails—be sure to drill pilot holes for the nails.

FINISH THE WOOD. For cleanest results, perform the finishing steps on the table prior to installing the ceramic tile. Start by filling all open counterbore holes with ⅜"-dia. oak wood plugs **(photo D).** Finish-sand

the entire coffee table and apply sanding sealer to all exposed surfaces, except the top panel. Let the sealer dry thoroughly, then lightly sand the sealed surfaces with 180- or 220 grit sandpaper. Apply stain to the sealed oak surfaces, if desired, then apply two or three light coats of polyurethane to the wood.

INSTALL THE CERAMIC TOP. Once the finish has dried, the ceramic tiles can be installed. Start by masking off the top edges of the skirts to further protect the finished surfaces. Test-fit the table tiles (I), then apply a ⅛"-thick layer of tile adhesive over the entire table surface, using a V-notched adhesive trowel. Line the borders of the table surface with plastic spacers (we used 3/16" spacers with 6" ceramic wall tile to make a tabletop surface that fits inside the tabletop frame). Begin setting tiles into the adhesive, working in straight lines. Insert plastic spacers between tiles to maintain an even gap. Rap each tile lightly with a rubber mallet to set it into the adhesive **(photo E).** Once the tiles have been set in

place, remove the spacers and let the adhesive set overnight. Then, apply a layer of grout (we used pretinted grout that matches the color of the tile we chose) to the tile surface so it fills the gaps between tiles **(photo F).** Wipe any excess grout from the tile faces. Let grout dry for about 30 minutes (check manufacturer's directions first), then wipe off the grout film from the tiles with a damp sponge, wiping diagonally across the grout lines. Let the grout set for at least a week, then apply silicone grout sealer to the grout lines.

Use a grout float to apply tile grout in the gaps between tiles in the tabletop.

China Cabinet

This tall, sleek fixture displays and stores fine china and other housewares without occupying a lot of floor space.

PROJECT
POWER TOOLS

This modern-looking china cabinet features a snappy, efficient design to showcase and store all types of china and dishware with equal elegance. The bottom half of the cabinet is a simple cupboard for storing everyday serving trays, napkins, silverware and miscellaneous houseware.

The upper half is an open rack for displaying your favorite porcelain statues, china, vases and collectibles.

Among the more interesting features of this china cabinet are the 1" dowel columns that support the shelves in the rack area. The asymmetrical design allows you to store and display a wider range of items than if the cabinet was equally weighted on the right and left. And the overall slenderness of the cabinet means you can fit it

into just about any room, whether it's tucked into a corner or featured prominently along the center of a wall.

Plates and other items that are displayed in the rack area of the cabinet can be accentuated with plateholders. Or, you can do as we did and build a few custom-sized plate holders from scraps of molding. Just cut the molding into strips about the same width as the plates, and inset the strips at ¼" intervals in a plain wood frame.

CONSTRUCTION MATERIALS

Quantity	Lumber
2	¾" × 4 × 8' birch plywood
2	1"-dia. × 3' dowel
1	½ × ½ " × 3' quarter-round molding

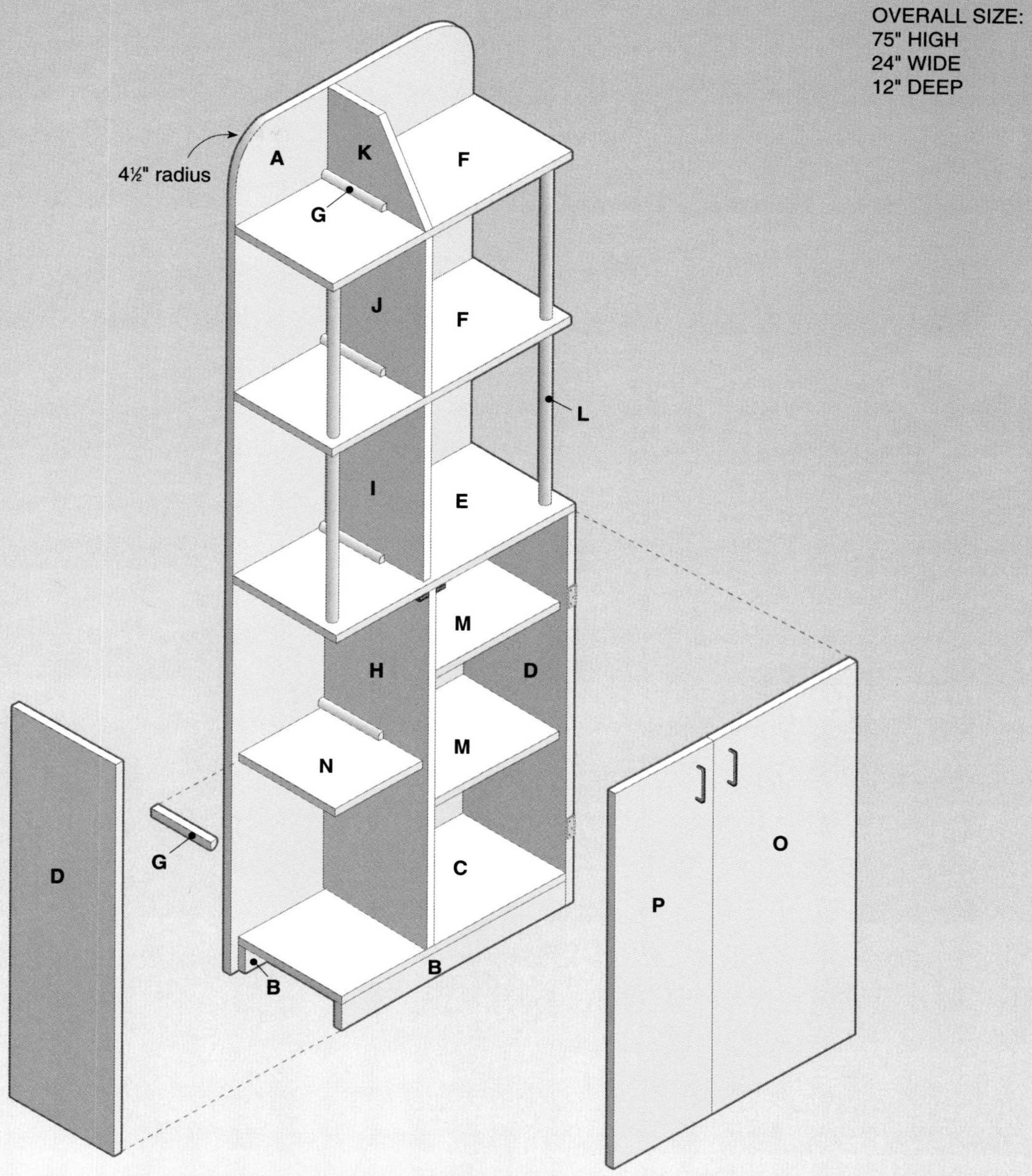

OVERALL SIZE:
75" HIGH
24" WIDE
12" DEEP

4½" radius

A K F
G
F
L
J
I E
M
H D
N M
G C
D
B B B
P O

Cutting List

Key	Part	Dimension	Pcs.	Material
A	Back	¾ × 24 × 75"	1	Plywood
B	Bottom rail	¾ × 2¼ × 22½"	2	Plywood
C	Cupboard bottom	¾ × 10½ × 22½"	1	Plywood
D	Cupboard side	¾ × 10½ × 35¼"	2	Plywood
E	Cupboard top	¾ × 10½ × 24"	1	Plywood
F	Rack shelf	¾ × 10 × 24"	2	Plywood
G	Cleat	½ × ½ × 6"	6	Toe molding
H	Cupboard divider	¾ × 10 × 32¼"	1	Plywood

Cutting List

Key	Part	Dimension	Pcs.	Material
I	Rack divider	¾ × 10 × 15⅛"	1	Plywood
J	Rack divider	¾ × 10 × 14¾"	1	Plywood
K	Rack divider	¾ × 8 × 7½"	1	Plywood
L	Column	1 × 30⅝"	2	Dowel
M	Cupboard shelf	¾ × 13¼ × 10"	2	Plywood
N	Cupboard shelf	¾ × 8½ × 10"	1	Plywood
O	Large door	¾ × 14¼ × 33¾"	1	Plywood
P	Small door	¾ × 9⅜ × 33¾"	1	Plywood

Materials: Wood glue, wood screws (#6 × 1¼", #6 × 2"), birch veneer edge tape (50'), ⅜"-dia. birch wood plugs, 1¼" brass butt hinges (4), 1¼" brads, magnetic door catches (2), 2½" brass door pulls (2), finishing materials.

Note: Measurements reflect the actual size of dimensional lumber.

Attach the cupboard bottom by driving screws through the cupboard sides and into the edges.

Carefully sand the wood plugs to level, using a belt sander or power hand sander.

Directions: China Cabinet

MAKE THE BACK PANEL. With its rounded top, the back panel runs the entire height of the china cabinet, anchoring both the rack and cupboard units. Start by cutting the back (A) to size. Sand this and all parts to smooth out rough spots after cutting. Use a compass to draw a semicircle roundover with a 4½" radius at each top corner of the back panel. Cut the curves with a jig saw. Use a household iron to apply birch veneer edge tape to the side and top edges of the back. Trim the excess tape with a sharp utility knife, then sand the edges smooth. As a guide for installing the rack shelves, mark reference points 52¾" and 67½" up from the bottom edge, 9¼" in from one side edge of the workpiece (this side should become the left side when facing from the front).

MAKE THE CUPBOARD. Start by cutting the bottom rails (B) and cupboard bottom (C) to size. Apply edge tape to one long edge of the cupboard bottom. Position the bottom rails beneath the cupboard bottom, flush with the edges. Drill counterbored pilot holes through the cupboard bottom and into the tops of the rails, then attach the parts with glue and #6 × 2" wood screws. Cut the cupboard sides (D) to size, and apply edge tape to the front edges. Position the cupboard bottom between the cupboard sides. Drill counterbored pilot holes, then apply glue and drive wood screws through the sides and into the edges of the cupboard bottom **(photo A).** Cut the cupboard top (E) to size, and apply edge tape to the front and side edges. Attach it to the tops of the cupboard sides with glue and screws driven down through the cupboard top and into the tops of the sides.

ATTACH CUPBOARD SHELVES & DIVIDER. Cut the cupboard divider (H) and cupboard shelves (M, N) to size. Apply veneer tape to the front edges

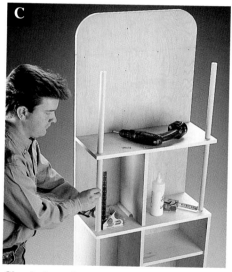

Check the columns for square before attaching them to the cabinet top.

of all shelves. Draw reference lines on the cupboard bottom and cupboard top, 9¼" in from the left cupboard side, for positioning the divider between them (these lines should align with the marks you made earlier on the back panel). Set the divider between the cupboard top and bottom, so the left face is aligned with the reference lines. Attach the divider with glue and wood screws, driven through the top and bottom and into the divider. Draw reference lines on the right side and right face of the divider, 12" and 24" up from the bottoms, for positioning the larger cupboard shelves (M). Draw reference lines for the smaller cupboard shelf (N) 16" up from the bottoms on the left side and left face of the divider. Apply glue to the side edges of all three shelves and position them between the cupboard sides and the divider, with their bottoms on the reference lines. Make sure the back edges of the shelves are flush with the back edges of the sides. Fasten the shelves with #6 × 2" wood screws, driven through the sides and the divider, and into the edges of the shelves. Glue ⅜"-dia. birch wood plugs into all the exposed counterbores in the cupboard. When the glue has dried, sand the plugs down to the surface of the plywood with a belt sander and a medium sanding belt **(photo B).** Be careful not to scar the surrounding wood. Attach the back panel to the cupboard with glue and #6 × 2" wood screws.

MAKE & MARK THE RACK PARTS. Cut the rack dividers (I, J, K) to full size. The lower rack dividers (I, J) are left square. The upper divider is trimmed off at an angle on the front edge. To make the angled cut in the upper divider, mark a point on one long edge, 5¼" from one end. Draw a straight line from that point to the bottom corner on the opposite end. Cut along the line with a jig saw or circular saw. Cut the two rack shelves (F) to size, sand smooth, then attach veneer edge tape to the front edges of the rack dividers, and to the front and side edges of

the rack shelves. With the taped edges facing you, draw reference lines on the shelves, 9¼" in from the left sides. Next, drill two 1"-dia. holes for the columns (L) all the way through one shelf. The center of each hole should be 1¾" in from the front edge and 1¼" in from the side edge of the shelf. This shelf will become the lower rack shelf. Cut the columns (L) to length.

INSTALL THE RACK. When installing the rack, alternate between shelves and dividers. Use glue and #6 × 2" wood screws, driven through counterbored pilot holes in the back panel, to fasten the lower rack divider (I) in position at the marks on the shelf and back panel. Use a square to make sure the divider is perpendicular to the back panel. Cut cleats from quarter-round molding (G) to size, and use glue and 1¼" brads to attach the cleats on each side of the divider, flush against the back. Apply glue to the top edge of the lower divider, and position the shelf with the 1"-dia. holes on top of the divider, so the holes are in front. Attach the shelf to the divider with wood screws, driven through the back and into the shelf, and through the shelf and into the lower divider. Apply glue to the bottom of each column, and slide them through the holes in the shelf. Use a square to make sure they are straight **(photo C),** then drive a #6 × 1¼" wood screw up through the cabinet top and into the bottom of each column. Next, position the middle rack divider (J) on the shelf. Fasten it with glue, screws and cleats. Attach the upper shelf to the middle

divider and back panel with glue and wood screws, then drive #6 × 1¼" wood screws through the shelf and into the tops of the columns. Finally, apply glue to the back and bottom edges of the upper divider, and attach it with wood screws and cleats.

INSTALL THE DOORS. Start by cutting the doors (O, P) to size. Apply edge tape to all edges of each door. Make sure all the surfaces are sanded smooth. Attach 1¼" brass butt hinges to the doors, 3½" down from the top edges, and ½" up from the bottom edges. Fasten the doors to the cupboard sides, flush with the cabinet top **(photo D).** Install magnetic door catches on the cupboard divider and doors. Attach door pulls to the outside faces of the doors, 1½" down from the top edges of the doors, and 1½" in from the inside edges—we used plain, 2½" brass door pulls. Give the project a final finish-sanding, wipe clean with a rag dipped in mineral spirits, then apply your finish of choice (we simply applied two coats of polyurethane over unstained wood).

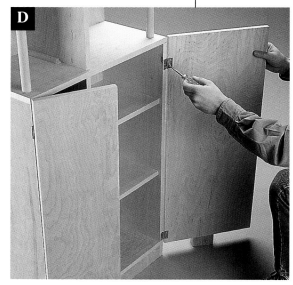

Hang the doors with brass butt hinges.

PROJECT
POWER TOOLS

Armoire

*With a simple, rustic appearance, this movable closet
can blend into almost any bedroom.*

CONSTRUCTION MATERIALS

Quantity	Lumber
3	¾" × 4 × 8' birch plywood
1	1 × 2" × 8' pine
6	1 × 3" × 8' pine
1	1 × 6" × 8' pine
1	1½"-dia. × 2' fir dowel

Long before massive walk-in closets became almost standard in residential building design, homeowners and apartment-dwellers compensated for cramped bedroom closets by making or buying an armoire. The trim armoire design shown here reflects the basic styling developed during the heyday of the armoire, but at a scale that makes it usable in just about any living situation. A mere 60" high and only 36" in width, this cute little armoire still boasts plenty of interior space. Five shelves on the left side are sized to store folded sweaters and shirts. And you can hang dozens of suit jackets or dresses in the closet section to the right.

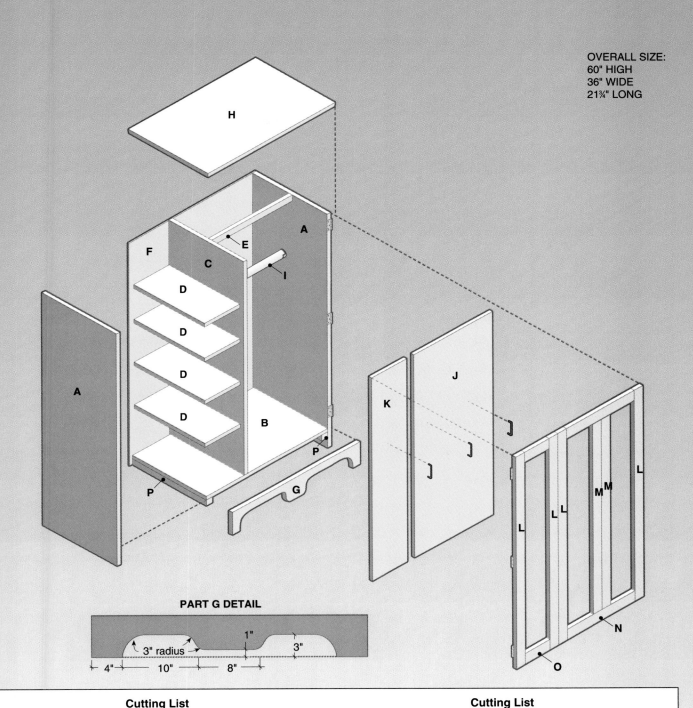

OVERALL SIZE:
60" HIGH
36" WIDE
21¾" LONG

PART G DETAIL

1"
3" radius
3"
4"
10"
8"

Cutting List

Key	Part	Dimension	Pcs.	Material
A	Side Panel	¾ × 21 × 59¼"	2	Birch Plywood
B	Bottom Panel	¾ × 21 × 34½"	1	Birch Plywood
C	Center Panel	¾ × 21 × 53¾"	1	Birch Plywood
D	Shelf	¾ × 10⅞ × 20¼"	4	Birch Plywood
E	Stringer	¾ × 1½ × 22¾"	1	Pine
F	Back	¼ × 34½ × 54½"	1	Birch Plywood
G	Front Skirt	¾ × 5½ × 36"	1	Pine
H	Top Panel	¾ × 22 × 36"	1	Birch Plywood

Cutting List

Key	Part	Dimension	Pcs.	Material
I	Closet Rod	1½ × 22¾"	1	Fir
J	Closet Door Panel	¾ × 22 × 48⅝"	1	Birch Plywood
K	Shelf Door Panel	¾ × 10 × 48⅝"	1	Birch Plywood
L	Door Stile	¾ × 2½ × 53⅝"	4	Pine
M	False Stile	¾ × 2½ × 48⅝"	2	Pine
N	Closet Door Rail	¾ × 2½ × 18¹⁵⁄₁₆"	2	Pine
O	Shelf Door Rail	¾ × 2½ × 6¹⁵⁄₁₆"	2	Pine
P	Cleat	¾ × 1½ × 21"	2	Pine

Materials: #6 × 1½" wood screws, finish nails (3d, 6d), wood glue, closet rod hangers, ¾" birch edge tape (50'), wrought iron hinges and pulls, finishing materials.
Note: Measurements reflect the actual thickness of dimensional lumber.

Apply veneer edge tape to the exposed plywood edges so they can be stained. Trim off excess tape with a sharp utility knife.

Directions: Armoire

PREPARE THE PLYWOOD PANELS. Careful preparation of the plywood panels used to make the sides, bottom, top and shelves is key to creating an armoire with a clean, professional look. Take the time to make sure all the parts are precisely square, then apply self-adhesive veneer edge tape to all plywood edges that will be visible (if you plan to paint the armoire, you can simply fill the edges with wood putty, then sand them smooth before you apply the paint). Cut the side panels (A), bottom panel (B) center panel (C), and shelves (D) to size from ¾"-thick plywood, using a circular saw and straightedge cutting guide. We used birch plywood because it is easy to work with and takes wood stain well. Smooth the edges and surfaces of the panels with medium sandpaper. Apply self-adhesive veneer edge tape to the front edges of the center panel, side panels and shelves. An effective way to apply self-adhesive edge tape is to cut it into strips, position the strips over the edges, then press them with a household iron set on low-to-medium heat setting. The heat from the iron activates the adhesive. Press all the edge tape strips into place. When the adhesive has cooled and set, trim the excess edge tape with a sharp utility knife **(photo A).** Sand the trimmed edges and surfaces of the edge tape with medium sandpaper.

ASSEMBLE THE CARCASE. The *carcase* for the armoire (or any type of cabinet) is the main cabinet box. For this project,

Clamp the bottom panel between the sides and fasten to the cleats with 6d finish nails and glue.

Fasten the shelves between the side panel and center panel with glue and 6d finish nails.

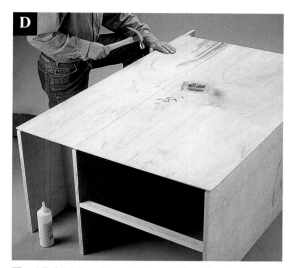

The ¼"-thick back panel is nailed to the back edges of the carcase to help keep it in square.

Lay out the decorative cutout at the bottom of the front skirt board using a compass to make the curves, then cut with a jig saw.

the carcase includes the sides, bottom and center panel. The panels are fastened together with wood glue and finish nails. Make sure all the joints are square and the edges are flush. Start by laying out the cleat positions on the lower sections of the side panels. Measure up 4¾" from the bottom edges of the side panels and draw a layout line across each side panel. Cut the cleats (P) to length from 1 × 2 pine, place them just below the layout lines, and secure them in place with glue and 6d finish nails driven through the cleats and into the side panels. Then, stand the side panels upright on their bottom edges and apply a bead of wood glue to the top of each cleat. Place the bottom panel between the side panels on top of the cleats, then clamp in place. Make sure the taped front edges of the side panels are flush and in alignment. Drive 6d finish nails through the bottom panel and into each cleat, then drive nails through the side panels and into the edges of the bottom panel. Fasten the bottom panel

to the cleats and side panels with 6d finish nails **(photo B).** Set all nail heads with a nail set. Next, lay the assembly on its back edge. Use a pair of shelves as spacers to set the correct distance between the center panel and the left side panel (as seen from the front of the carcase). Make sure the taped panel edges are at the front of the project. Fasten the center panel to the bottom panel with glue and finish nails.

INSTALL THE SHELVES. Mark shelf position reference lines on the inside face of the left side panel and on the left face of the center panel. Measure up from the top of the bottom panel and draw lines at 12", 22¾", 33½", and 42¼". Use a carpenter's square to make sure the lines are perpendicular to the front and back edges of the panels. Arrange the shelves (D) so the tops are just below the reference lines, flush with the back edges of the carcase (creating a recess in front of each shelf). Attach the shelves with glue

and 6d finish nails driven through the side panel and center panel, and into the edges of the shelves **(photo C).** Brace each panel from behind as you drive the nails. Set all nail heads.

ATTACH THE STRINGER & BACK PANEL. Cut the stringer (E) to length from 1 × 2 pine and fasten it between the center panel and side panel with glue and 6d finish nails. The stringer should be centered between the fronts and backs of the panels, and flush with the tops. Cut the back panel (F) to size from ¼" birch plywood. Measure the distances between opposite corners of the carcase to make sure it is square (the distances between corners should be equal). Adjust the carcase as needed, then position the back panel over the back edges of the carcase so the edges of the back panel are flush with the outside faces of the side panels. Fasten the back panel by driving 3d finish nails through the back and into the edges of the side, center and bottom panels, using 3d finish nails **(photo D).**

Mount the top panel so it covers the top edge of the back panel, and overhangs the front edges of the side panels by ¾".

Strips of 1 × 3 are attached to the fronts of the door panels to create a frame.

MAKE & ATTACH THE FRONT SKIRT. The front skirt serves as a decorative accent at the bottom of the armoire, and also conceals the empty space below the bottom panel. Start the skirt construction by cutting the front skirt (G) to length from 1 × 6 pine. To lay out the curves that form the ends of the decorative cutouts on the skirt board (see *Diagram*, page 25), start by measuring in 7" from each end and using a compass to draw a 3"-radius curve at each point to make the outside end of each cutout. Then, measure 11¾" in from each end of the skirt board and draw a 3"-radius curve to mark the top, inside end of each cutout. Measure 16⅜" in from each end of the skirt board, and mark points that are 1¾" down from the top edge of the board. Set the point of your compass at each of these points and draw curves that mark the bottom, inside ends of the cutouts. Then, at the middle of the bottom edge of the board,

measure up 1" and draw a line parallel to the bottom edge, intersecting the inside ends of the cutout lines. Finally, draw lines parallel to the bottom edge of the board, 3" up, to create the top of each cutout. Make the cutout on the skirt board, using a jig saw **(photo E).** Smooth the jig saw cuts with medium sandpaper. Position the skirt board against the front of the armoire carcase to make sure that the ends of the skirt are flush with the outside surfaces of the side panels, and the top of the skirt is flush with the top of the bottom panel. Fasten the front skirt to the front edges of the side panels and bottom panel with glue and 6d finish nails.

MAKE & ATTACH THE TOP PANEL. Stand the armoire upright, and measure the distance between the outside faces of the side panels (it should be 36"). Cut the top panel (H) so it matches that distance in length, and is 22" wide. Test-fit the top panel to make sure the

edges are flush with the outside faces of the side panels. The back edge should be flush with the back panel, and the front edge of the top should overhang the front of the carcase panels by ¾". Apply veneer edge tape to all four edges of the top panel (see *Prepare the Plywood Panels,* page 26). Fasten the top panel to the center panel, side panels and stringer with glue and 6d finish nails **(photo F),** making sure it is in the same position as it was when you test-fit the part.

BUILD THE DOORS. The doors are designed for easy construction, durable service and attractive appearance. They are simply plywood panels with pine trim surrounding the perimeter of each door panel. Start the door construction by cutting the closet door panel (J) and shelf door panel (K) to size from ¾"-thick plywood. Sand the edges and surfaces of the door panels to smooth out the saw blade marks and any rough spots. Apply edge tape to

Hang the armoire doors with pairs of hinges attached to the door stiles and to the front edges of the side panels.

the edges of each door panel, then trim off the excess and sand the edges smooth. Next, cut the door stiles (L), false stiles (M), closet door rails (N) and shelf door rails (O) to length from 1 × 3 pine (*rails* are the horizontal frame pieces, *stiles* are vertical frame pieces). Position the rails and stiles on the door panels so they over-hang the door panels by ¾" at all edges of the panels. Tack the rails and stiles in place on both door panels with glue and 3d finish nails. Turn the door panels over on a worksurface, then reinforce the joints be-tween the stiles and rails and the door panels with counter-sunk #6 × 1½" wood screws driven through the counter-sunk pilot holes in the door panels, and into the stiles and rails **(photo G).** To hang the doors, first mark points along the outside edge of each outer door stile, 8" down from the top and 8" up from the bottom. Mount door hinges to the edges

of the stiles at these points (we used wrought-iron hinges). With the hinges mounted to the doors, position the doors in place against the side panels and fasten the hinges to the side panels **(photo H).** Be sure to adjust the hinges to allow for ⅛"-wide gaps between the door frames and the top panel, and between the doors.

APPLY THE FINISH. It is easier if you finish the parts of the ar-moire before you attach the rest of the hardware. Start by filling all nail holes and screw countersink holes with untinted wood putty, then sand the dried putty so it is smooth and even with the wood surface. Sand all the wood surfaces with medium (150-grit) sandpaper. Finish-sand the surfaces with fine sandpaper (180-or 220-grit), using a hand-held power sander. Wipe the wood clean, then brush on a coat of sand-ing sealer so the wood will accept the wood stain more evenly—be sure to read the directions and warnings on the

can label before applying any finishing products. Apply wood stain (if desired, you can also leave the wood unstained and simply apply a protective top-coat). Let the stain dry com-pletely, then apply several coats of topcoating product— we used two thin coats of water-based, satin polyurethane.

INSTALL THE HARDWARE. The final step in finishing the ar-moire is installing the door catches and door pulls and the closet rod. Install door pulls on the door panels, 25" up from each bottom rail and centered between the stiles—we used hammered wrought-iron pulls for a nice rustic look. Mount closet-rod hangers to the sides of the closet compartment, 11" down from the top panel. Cut a 1½"-dia. closet rod (I) to length, and slip it into the closet rod hangers (applying finishing materials to the closet rod is optional). Finally, install mag-netic door catches and catch plates on the upper corners of the doors and the correspond-ing areas on the bottom of the top panel to keep the doors closed tightly when not in use. For extra holding power, install catches at the bottoms of the doors as well.

TIP

An armoire is basically a free standing closet, but with a few modifications it can become a custom furnishing that meets a variety of specific needs. To bolster its use as a dressing cabinet, attach a full-length dressing mirror to the inside of one of the doors, rearrange the shelf positions and drill a few holes in the back, and you've got a beauti-ful entertainment center; or, add more shelves and tuck the armoire in your kitchen to become a portable pantry.

Portable Workbench

Turn a few square feet of floor space into an efficient workshop with this portable, fold-up workbench.

CONSTRUCTION MATERIALS

Quantity	Lumber
4	2 × 4" × 8' pine
2	¾" × 4 × 8' plywood

If your desire to build things is bigger than the space you have to work in, then an expandable, portable workbench may be just the solution you're looking for. Tucked away in a basement, garage or any spare room, this workbench keeps a low profile, while giving you a place to store all of your tools. When the weekend rolls around, roll out the workbench, flip up the extension leaves at the ends of the worksurface, and you've got a workbench large enough to handle full 4 × 8 sheets of plywood and other big-scale building materials. Built from plywood, 2 × 4s and a few pieces of hardware, this workbench is quick and easy to make.

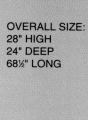

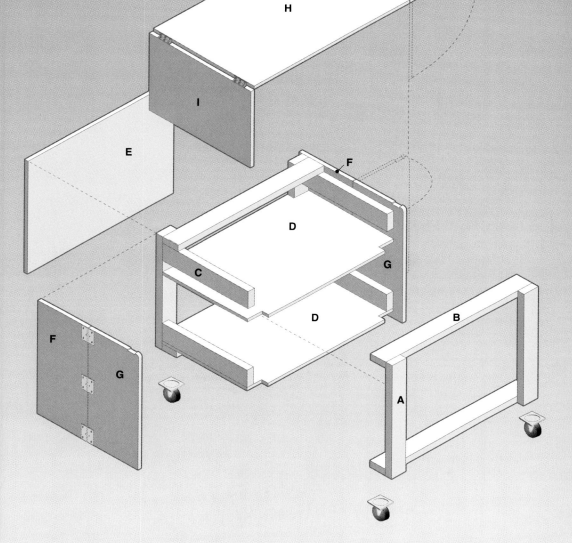

Cutting List

Key	Part	Dimension	Pcs.	Material
A	Leg	1½ × 3½ × 24¼"	4	Pine
B	Side rail	1½ × 3½ × 34½"	4	Pine
C	End rail	1½ × 3½ × 20¼"	4	Pine
D	Shelf	¾ × 23¼ × 34½"	2	Plywood
E	Back	¾ × 24¼ × 34½"	1	Plywood

Cutting List

Key	Part	Dimension	Pcs.	Material
F	End	¾ × 12 × 24¼"	2	Plywood
G	Door	¾ × 12 × 24¼"	2	Plywood
H	Top	¾ × 24 × 36½"	1	Plywood
I	Leaf	¾ × 16 × 24"	2	Plywood

Materials: Wood glue, wood screws (#6 × 1½", #6 × 2", #6 × 2½"), steel utility butt hinges (3 × 1½", 3 × 3"), 3" fixed casters (2), 3" swivel casters with brakes (2), finishing materials.

Note: Measurements reflect the actual size of dimensional lumber.

Check the frame assemblies to make sure they are square before you fasten them together.

Slide the shelf into place on the clamped spacers, 15¼" up from the bottoms of the legs.

Directions: Portable Workbench

MAKE THE FRONT & BACK FRAMES. The front and back of the workbench is made from two identical 2 × 4 frames, which are made by attaching side rails to the top and bottom of a pair of legs. Start by cutting the legs (A) and side rails (B) to size. Sand all parts to smooth out rough spots after cutting. Set a pair of side rails on edge on your worksurface. Position a leg on each end of the side rails, face up. The edges of the legs should be flush with the ends of the side rails. Use a framing square to make sure the legs are square to the side rails, and apply glue to the mating surfaces. Attach the legs to the side rails with #6 × 2½" wood screws, checking to make sure the parts are square as you work **(photo A).**

ATTACH THE END RAILS & SHELVES. The end rails and shelves fit between the front and back frames to form the cabinet section of the workbench. Each shelf is notched to fit between the legs. Cut the

Before attaching the top, make sure it overhangs the ends by ¼".

end rails (C) and shelves (D) to size. Use a jig saw to cut a 1½"-wide × 3½"-long notch at each corner of the shelves. For the notches to properly accommodate the legs, they should run lengthwise down the long edges of the shelves. Stand the leg sections up, and position a shelf between them on the bottom side rails. Make sure the

legs fit snugly in the shelf notches. Attach the shelf with #6 × 1¼" wood screws, driven through the shelf and into the side rails. Set one end rail on edge at each end of the shelf, flush with the outside edges of the legs. Attach the end rails with wood glue and #6 × 2½" wood screws, driven through the legs and into the end rails.

Dip wood screws in epoxy to fortify the holding power when the screws are being driven into the edges of plywood.

Position the unattached end rails underneath the top side rails, flush with their outside edges (see *Diagram*, page 31). Attach the end rails with glue and wood screws. Mark reference lines on the inside faces of the legs, 15¼" up from the leg bottoms. Clamp scrap blocks to the inside faces of the legs on the reference lines, and slide the remaining shelf into place so it rests on the scrap blocks **(photo B).** Use a combination square to make sure the shelf is square with the legs. If the shelf isn't square with the legs, adjust the height of the scrap blocks as needed. Secure the shelf by driving 2½" wood screws through the legs and into the shelf. Remove the scrap blocks.

ATTACH THE BACK, ENDS & TOP. Start by cutting the back (E), ends (F) and top (H) to size. Position the back against one long side of the assembled frame. The edges of the back should be flush with the edges of the legs. Attach one end of the back to one leg, using #6 × 2" wood screws. Check the workbench frame to make sure it is square. Drive evenly

spaced, #6 × 1¼" wood screws through the back and into the middle shelf. Position an end on each side of the workbench, flush with the bottoms of the rear legs. The back and ends should meet at the corners, with the rear edge of each end flush with the rear face of the back. Fasten the ends with #6 ×1¼" wood screws. Center the top onto the workbench, and check to make sure it overhangs each end by ¼" **(photo C).** Apply glue to the tops of the side rails, then secure the top by driving #6 × 2" wood screws through the top and into the side rails. Countersink the screws in the top to recess the screw heads.

ATTACH THE DOORS & LEAVES. The workbench doors are attached to the ends with hinges. The doors swing out to support the leaves, which are attached to the top with hinges. Begin by cutting the doors (G) and leaves (I) to size. To allow the doors to swing clear of the hinges for the leaves, make a 3½"-long notch on the top edge of each door with a jig saw. Start each notch 1¼" from the

front edge of the door (the notches only need to be about ¼" deep). Smooth over the front corners and edges of the doors with a sander. Attach 3 × 3" steel utility hinges at the top and bottom of each door, then attach them to the ends, keeping the top and bottom edges flush. Next, fasten 3 × 1½" steel utility hinges to one long edge of each leaf, 1½" in from the front and back ends. The barrels of the hinges should hang slightly below the bottoms of the leaves. Attach the leaves to the edges of the top with the hinges. When driving screws into the end grain of plywood, apply epoxy glue to the screws before driving them **(photo D).** The epoxy glue creates a very strong, permanent bond for the screws. Because the bond is permanent, make sure you dry-fit the parts before applying the epoxy glue.

APPLY FINISHING TOUCHES. For ease of steering, use a combination of fixed and swivelling casters (this is a little like the wheels on a car: the rear wheels are fixed parallel to the car frame, and the front wheels pivot to steer the car). Attach heavy-duty, 3" fixed (non-swiveling) casters to the bottoms of the legs at one end of the workbench. Attach 3" swiveling, locking casters to the legs at the other end of the workbench. Center the casters on the legs. Fill the screw holes in the top with wood putty, and paint all surfaces with primer and enamel paint.

TIP

Epoxy glue is a two-part product that is usually sold in pairs of tubes that look a little like a syringe. To use epoxy, squirt a little of the material from each tube onto a mixing surface, then blend them together with a small stick. Use the blended epoxy immediately.

PROJECT
POWER TOOLS

Mirrored Display Shelf

*A wood-frame mirror creates the illusion of space
in this wall-hung display shelf.*

CONSTRUCTION MATERIALS

Quantity	Lumber
1	1 × 2" × 2' aspen
1	1 × 3" × 6' aspen
1	1 × 4" × 3' aspen
1	1 × 6" × 2' aspen

Turn empty wall space into a display area for curios or plants, and make the room look larger in the process. The mirrored back on this wood-frame display rack adds the illusion of depth to an otherwise smaller room, and the straightforward styling of the rack adds warmth and interest to the decor. The nar-row shelf that's attached to the lower rail of the mirror frame is wide enough to support curios, knicknacks or even small houseplants.

We used aspen to build this mirrored display rack because it is hard and durable, and it looks good when stained. You can use oak or just about any other hardwood, if you prefer.

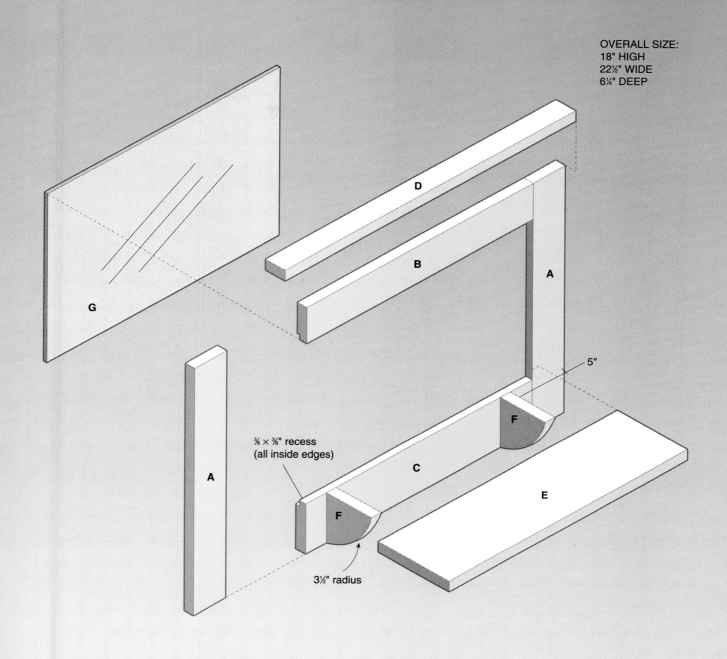

OVERALL SIZE:
18" HIGH
22½" WIDE
6¼" DEEP

⅜ × ⅜" recess
(all inside edges)

3½" radius

5"

Cutting List

Key	Part	Dimension	Pcs.	Material
A	Frame Stile	¾ × 2½ × 17¼"	2	Aspen
B	Top Rail	¾ × 2½ × 17½"	1	Aspen
C	Bottom Rail	¾ × 3½ × 17½"	1	Aspen
D	Cap	¾ × 1½ × 22½"	1	Aspen

Cutting List

Key	Part	Dimension	Pcs.	Material
E	Shelf	¾ × 5½ × 18½"	1	Aspen
F	Shelf Support	¾ × 3½ × 3½"	2	Aspen
G	Mirror	¼ × 11¾ × 18"	1	Mirror

Materials: Wood glue, wood screws (#6 × 1½", #8 × 3"), ⅜"-dia. wood plugs.

Note: Measurements reflect the actual thickness of dimensional lumber.

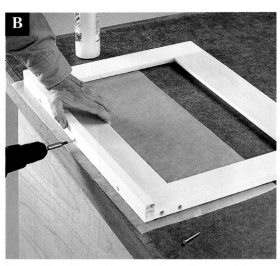

Make plain butt joints at the corners of the frame, reinforced with glue and 3" wood screws. Make sure the screws are driven straight.

Fasten the decorative cap strip to the top of the frame with glue and 1½" wood screws.

Directions: Mirrored Display Shelf

BUILD THE MIRROR FRAME. The mirror in this project is housed in a wooden frame made with simple butt joints that are reinforced with screws and glue. When it's time to drill the pilot holes for the screws, use a portable drill guide, if you have one, to make sure the holes are centered in the boards. Start the frame construction by cutting the frame stiles (A) and top rail (B) to length from 1 × 3 wood. Then, cut the bottom rail (C) to length from a 1 × 4. Sand the edges and surfaces with medium-grit sandpaper to smooth out any rough spots. Next, lay the rails and stiles on a flat worksurface, with the rails between the stiles, to form a rectangular frame. Keep the outside edges of the rails flush with the ends of the stiles. Clamp the rails between the stiles with a pipe clamp or bar clamp to securely hold them in place. Be sure to clamp in the middle of the stiles to allow room for counterboring and

fastening toward the ends of the stiles. Use scrap wood or clamp shoes to protect the edges of the frame boards from damage from the clamps. Drill pilot holes for #8 × 3" wood screws through the stiles into the ends of the rails. It's important to keep the drill level and straight when boring deep holes. Counterbore the pilot holes to accept ⅜"-dia. wood plugs. When all holes have been counterbored, unclamp the frame and apply glue to the ends of the rails and the portions of the stile edge that will be in contact with the rail ends. Clamp the frame, and fasten the stiles to the rails with #8 × 3" wood screws **(photo A).**

CUT THE MIRROR RECESS. The ¼"-thick mirror for the display shelf is set into a groove, called a rabbet, that is cut around the inside edges of the frame at the back. The easiest tool for making these cuts is a router with a self-piloted rabbet bit that follows edges of the board to guide the cuts. After making the rabbet cut, you'll need to go in with a wood chisel and square off the rounded ends of

the cuts. Mount a ⅜"-dia. rabbet bit in your router, and set the cutting depth for ⅜". Clamp the frame securely to your worksurface, with the back side up. Cut a ⅜ × ⅜" rabbet groove around the inside perimeter of the frame, then square off the cut with a wood chisel.

ATTACH THE FRAME CAP. The frame cap is a plain strip of wood installed as a decorative element that is attached to the top rail of the frame. Start by cutting the cap (D) to length from 1 × 2 wood. Sand the edges and surfaces with medium-grit sandpaper to smooth out any rough spots. Position the cap along the top rail with its ends flush with the edges of the stiles, and clamp it in place. Drill counterbored pilot holes for #6 × 1½" wood screws through the cap and into the top rail. Remove the clamps, and apply glue to the top edge of the frame assembly and the surface area of the cap that contacts the top rail. Reposition the cap against the rail, and fasten the cap to the top rail with 1½" wood screws **(photo B).**

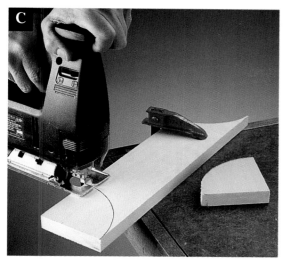

Draw an arc with a 3½" radius on a 1 × 4 to outline a shelf support, then cut out with a jig saw.

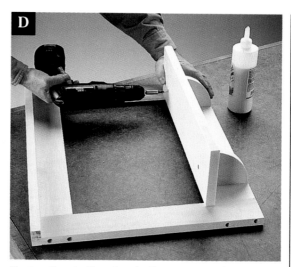

Fasten the shelf to the shelf supports with 1½" screws driven through counterbored pilot holes.

ATTACH THE SHELF SUPPORTS. The display shelf is installed even with the bottom of the frame opening, and supported by rounded shelf supports that you'll make with a jig saw and attach to the bottom frame rail. Draw outlines for the shelf supports (F) on a piece of 1 × 4 wood. First, measure 3½" along one edge and place a mark. Use a compass to draw an arc with a 3½" radius from the mark to the opposite corner. Cut out the shelf support using a jig saw **(photo C).** Sand the edges smooth. Then, lay the shelf support back on the 1 × 4, and use it as a template to trace the outline for an identical shelf support. Cut and sand smooth the second shelf support. Next, mark the shelf support positions on the bottom rail so the outer edges of the shelf supports are 5" in from the edges of the frame. Set the supports against the lines, and trace the inside edge of each support to form an outline. Remove the supports, and mark pilot hole drilling points 1" and 2½" up from the bottom edge of the bottom rail, centered in each support outline. Drill pilot holes through the centerpoints, countersinking the holes at the back side of the frame so the screw heads will not stick out. Reposition the supports in the outlines, and extend the pilot holes in the frame into the ends of the supports. Attach the supports with glue and #6 × 1½" wood screws driven through the back of the frame and into the ends of the supports **(photo D).**

ATTACH THE SHELF. Start by cutting the shelf (E) to length from 1 × 6 wood. Set the shelf on the shelf supports so the back edge is flush with the face of the frame, and the ends are flush with the outside edges of the frame. Attach the shelf to the shelf supports with glue and a pair of #6 × 1½" wood screws driven through counterbored pilot holes in the shelf and down into the supports.

APPLY FINISHING TOUCHES. Glue ⅜"-dia. wood plugs in all counterbores, and sand them so they are even with the wood surface. Smooth out any sharp edges, and finish-sand all surfaces with fine (180-or 220-grit) sandpaper. Apply wood stain (if desired) to the surfaces, following the manufacturer's directions. Apply a topcoat (we used two light coats of polyurethane). Have the mirror (G) cut to size at a hardware or glass supply store, and insert it into the recess in the back of the frame. Secure the mirror with mirror clips (a specialty fastener) or glazier's points.

HANG THE DISPLAY SHELF. To hang the mirrored display shelf on your wall, first use a stud finder to locate wall studs in the area. Mark the studs, then center the shelf across two studs and mark the stud positions on the top rail of the mirror. Drill a counterbored pilot hole for a #8 × 3" wood screw at each point, then position the shelf against the walls so the pilot holes are centered over the studs. Use a carpenter's level to make sure the shelf is level, then drive 3" screws through the pilot holes. Glue wood plugs into the counterbores, and stain and topcoat them to match the rest of the wood.

Bathroom Drying Rack

Station this drying rack in a bathroom corner for drying towels, or add the removable drying rods and set the rack in your tub or shower for drying fine washables.

PROJECT
POWER TOOLS

Finding a good spot for drying towels or hand-washed clothing is a real challenge in a typical small bathroom. This bathroom drying rack is designed to fit in your bathtub or shower stall, where it can be used to dry a whole drawerful of fine washables at one time. Or, with the removable drying rods stowed in the base, it can be set against a wall in your bathroom and used as a towel rack. While it may not be the centerpiece of your bathroom decor, it is definitely more interesting to look at than the average clothes rack.

This rack features three fixed rods from 18" to 36" in length that are aligned so the rack can fit neatly against a wall. The base has four storage holes for removable rods of various lengths that are inserted for extra drying capacity.

The pole that supports the drying rods is a 72" fluted wood curtain rod. Selection for curtain rods will vary, but look for one that is at least 1⅜" in diameter. The fluting gives the rack a nice design touch, while helping to channel water toward the round plywood base. For an additional decorative touch, we capped the pole with a wooden finial. We coated all the project pieces with glossy exterior paint for an attractive, water-resistant finish.

CONSTRUCTION MATERIALS

Quantity	Lumber
1	1⅜"-dia. × 6' wood pole
3	¾"-dia. × 6' dowel
1	¾" × 2 × 4' plywood
1	1⅜"-dia. ball finial

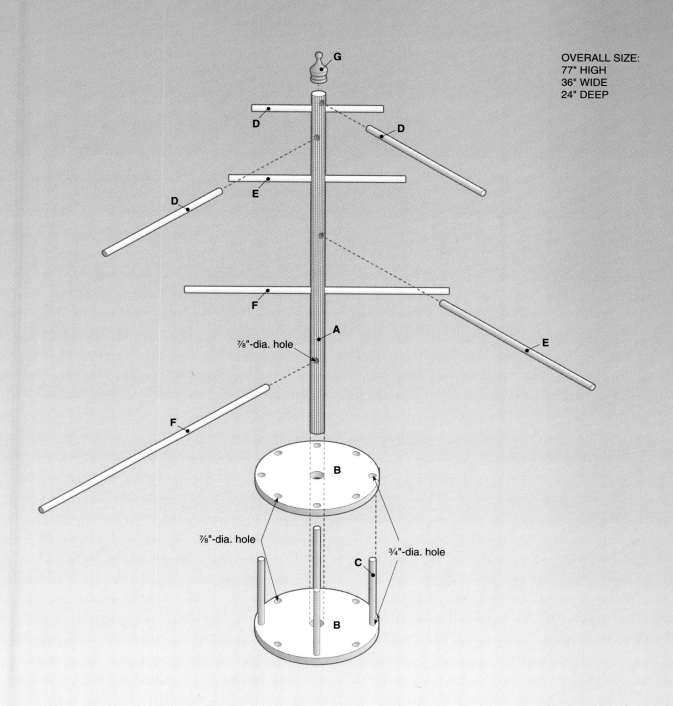

OVERALL SIZE:
77" HIGH
36" WIDE
24" DEEP

G

D

D

E

D

F

A

⅞"-dia. hole

E

F

⅞"-dia. hole

B

C

¾"-dia. hole

B

Cutting List				
Key	**Part**	**Dimension**	**Pcs.**	**Material**
A	Pole	1⅜"-dia. × 72"	1	Fluted pole
B	Base plate	¾ × 14"-dia.	2	Plywood
C	Base pillar	¾"-dia. × 10"	4	Dowel
D	Rod	¾"-dia. × 18"	3	Dowel

Cutting List				
Key	**Part**	**Dimension**	**Pcs.**	**Material**
E	Rod	¾"-dia. × 24"	2	Dowel
F	Rod	¾"-dia. × 36"	2	Dowel
G	Cap	1⅜"-dia. base	1	Ball finial

Materials: Moisture-resistant glue, #12 × 3" wood screw, 4d finish nails, rubber glide feet (4), finishing materials.

Note: Measurements reflect the actual size of dimensional lumber.

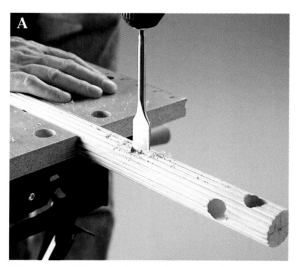

When you drill the holes for the removable rods, rotate the pole ¼ turn before drilling each hole.

Drive 4d finish nails through pilot holes in the base plates and into the dowel pillars to secure the parts.

Directions:
Bathroom Drying Rack

PREPARE THE POLE. We used a 48"-long, 1⅜"-dia. fluted wood curtain rod in this drying rack project. To accept the ¾"-dia. permanent drying rods, drill ¾"-dia. holes through the pole at three points. For the four removable rods, drill ⅞"-dia. holes. Start by drilling the holes for the fixed rods. Lay the pole flat on your worksurface and clamp it in place. Designate one end as the top, and measure and mark points 2", 12", and 28" down from the top, making sure the points are aligned along a vertical line running the length of the pole. Using the points as drilling points, drill ¾"-dia. holes at all three locations with a ¾"-dia. spade bit. To ensure that the holes are straight and parallel to one another, use a portable drill guide attachment on your drill. The four guide holes for the removable rods should be staggered so they are not parallel to one another or to the holes for the fixed rods. To accomplish this, rotate the post ¼

turn before drilling each hole. Drill the ⅞"-dia. holes at points 1", 6", 20", and 38" down from the top, rotating the pole ¼ turn before each hole is drilled **(photo A).** Sand around the edges of the holes to remove any rough spots. After the holes are drilled, attach a decorative finial to the top of the pole (in most cases, to install the finial you'll need to drill a centered pilot hole in the top of the pole, then insert the built-in screw in the finial and turn until secure).

MAKE THE BASE PLATES. The base plates are 14"-dia. round plywood cutouts with eight holes for ¾"-dia. dowels in each plate. Four of the holes will house permanent base pillars, and the other four will provide storage for the removable drying rods. Begin making the base plates by cutting two pieces of ¾"-thick plywood to 14" square. Measure and mark the midpoint of each edge of one of the plates (7"), then connect the lines on opposite sides with a straightedge. Next, draw lines connecting opposite corners of the plate—all lines should run through a single

centerpoint, dividing the plate into eight segments. Now, set the point of a compass at the centerpoint of the plate, and draw a pair of circles: one with a 5¾" radius, and one with a 7" radius. Attach or clamp the second plate directly beneath the marked plate. At the points where the inner circle intersects the lines, drill ¾"- and ⅞"-dia. holes through both plates (see *Diagram,* page 39). Then, use a jig saw to cut along the outer circle, forming two 14"-dia. parts. Sand any rough surfaces on the cutouts.

BUILD THE BASE. Select one of the base plates as the top plate, and cut a 1⅜"-dia. hole through the centerpoint, using a hole saw mounted in your electric drill. Lay the bottom base plate facedown on your worksurface. Find the centerpoint of the circle, and drill a ⅛"-dia. pilot hole for a #12 × 3" screw that will secure the post. Countersink the pilot hole so the screw head will be recessed. Cut a ¾"-dia. dowel into four 10"-long sections, and sand the ends smooth. Turn the bottom plate faceup on your

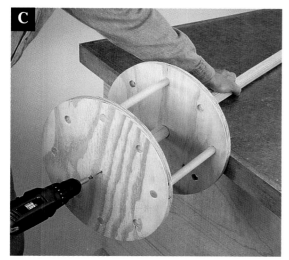

Drive a #12 × 3" wood screw through the bottom base plate and into the bottom of the pole.

Center the fixed rods in the holes and use 4d nails to secure them.

worksurface and clamp it in place. Apply moisture-resistant glue to one end of each of the four dowels. Insert a dowel into each ¾"-dia. hole in the base plate. Drill a pilot hole through the edge of the base plate and into each dowel, then drive a 4d finish nail through each pilot hole to secure the pillars **(photo B).** Clamp the top base plate to your worksurface, with the underside facing up. Apply glue to the free end of each dowel, then insert the dowels into guide holes in the top plate and secure them with finish nails. Also drive a 4d finish nail through the open holes in the bottom of the base to keep the removable rods from falling through when you lift the rack.

CUT RODS & PAINT ALL PARTS. Cut the fixed towel rods and removable drying rods (D, E, F) from ¾"-dia. doweling. Finish-sand the rods and all other parts, then paint them with exterior primer and glossy exterior paint.

INSTALL THE POLE IN THE BASE. Find the center of the bottom of the pole and mark a drilling point. Drill a ⅛"-dia.

pilot hole through the center-point. Insert the bottom of the pole in the 1⅜"-dia. hole in the top base plate, and check to make sure it is exactly vertical. Apply moisture-resistant glue to the bottom of the pole, then lay the base on its side and position the pole so the pilot hole in the bottom is aligned with the pilot hole in the center of the bottom base plate. Drive a #12 × 3" wood screw through the base and into the bottom of the pole **(photo C).** Attach rubber glide feet to the underside of each base pillar.

INSTALL THE FIXED RODS. Insert rods into the three holes drilled on the same plane into the pole (at 2", 12", and 28")— install an 18" rod in the top hole, then a 24" rod, then a 36" rod. Arrange the rods so the overhang is equal at each end, then drill a pilot hole through the pole and into each rod, and drive a 4d finish nail through each pilot hole to secure the rods **(photo D).** With only the fixed rods in place, the rack can be set against a wall in your bathroom and used as a towel rack. The removable

clothes rods are stored in the open holes in the base **(photo E).** To use the rack as a drying rack for clothes and delicate washables, set it in your bathtub or shower stall, and insert the removable rods into the holes (make sure the shorter rods are inserted higher up on the pole).

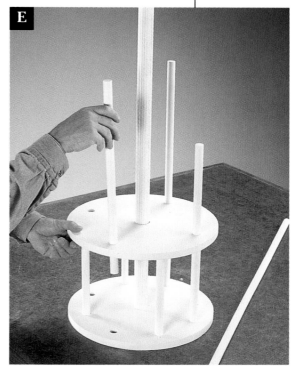

Store the removable rods in the base plates when not in use.

Nesting Office

*The basic building blocks of a home office, designed to
fit together in one small space.*

CONSTRUCTION MATERIALS

Quantity	Lumber
3	2 × 2" × 8' oak
4	1 × 4" × 8' oak
2	1 × 2" × 8' oak
4	¾" × 2 × 4' oak plywood
1	⅜ × 1¹⁄₁₆" × 6' oak stop molding
2	¾ × ¾" × 8' oak cove molding

The desk and credenza are the two principal furnishings needed in any home office. This nesting office pair features both components at full size, but because they fit together they can be stored in about the same amount of space as a standard medium-size desk. Made of oak and oak plywood, both pieces are well constructed and pleasing to the eye. The desk has a large writing surface, and the credenza is a versatile rolling storage cabinet with a hanging-file box, and shelves for storage of books, paper and other material. A flip-up top lets you use the credenza as an auxiliary writing or computer surface, and still store office supplies below.

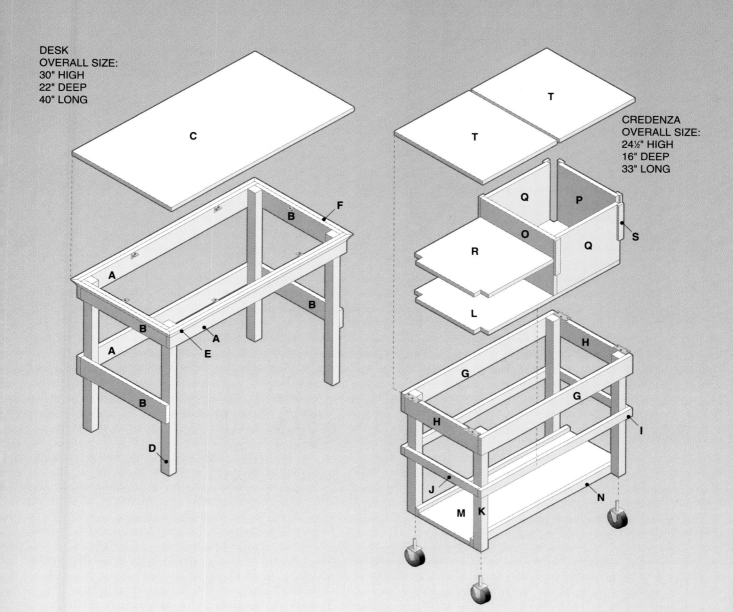

DESK
OVERALL SIZE:
30" HIGH
22" DEEP
40" LONG

CREDENZA
OVERALL SIZE:
24½" HIGH
16" DEEP
33" LONG

Cutting List				
Key	**Part**	**Dimension**	**Pcs.**	**Material**
A	Desk side	¾ × 3½ × 38"	3	Oak
B	Desk end	¾ × 3½ × 19"	4	Oak
C	Desk top	¾ × 22 × 40"	1	Plywood
D	Desk leg	1½ × 1½ × 29¼"	4	Oak
E	Side molding	¾ × ¾ × 40"	2	Cove molding
F	End molding	¾ × ¾ × 22"	2	Cove molding
G	Credenza side	¾ × 3½ × 33"	2	Oak
H	Credenza end	¾ × 3½ × 16"	2	Oak
I	Middle rail	¾ × 1½ × 33"	2	Oak
J	End rail	¾ × 1½ × 16"	2	Oak

Cutting List				
Key	**Part**	**Dimension**	**Pcs.**	**Material**
K	Credenza leg	1½ × 1½ × 21¼"	4	Oak
L	Middle shelf	¾ × 16 × 31½"	1	Plywood
M	Bottom shelf	¾ × 11½ × 31½"	1	Plywood
N	Bottom rail	¾ × 1½ × 31½"	2	Oak
O	Divider	¾ × 11¼ × 16"	1	Plywood
P	End panel	¾ × 11¼ × 13"	1	Plywood
Q	Side panel	¾ × 11¼ × 13⅞"	2	Plywood
R	Bin bottom	¾ × 15¼ × 16"	1	Plywood
S	Stop	⅜ × 1¹⁄₁₆ × 7"	6	Stop molding
T	Bin lid	¾ × 16⅜ × 19¼"	2	Plywood

Materials: Wood glue, #6 brass wood screws (¾", 1¼", 2"), 1¼" brass brads, 3 × 1½" brass hinges (4), 2½" swivel casters (4), ¾" oak edge tape (50'), 1¼" brass corner braces (6), brass lid supports (4), finishing materials.

Note: Measurements reflect the actual size of dimensional lumber.

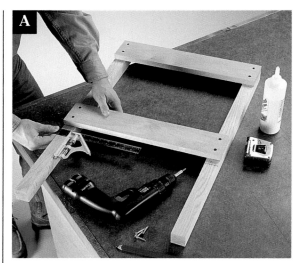

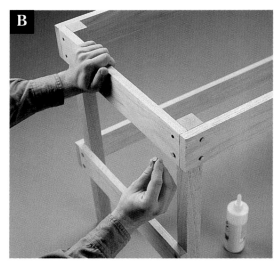

Double-check with a combination square to make sure the desk legs are square to the ends.

Oak plugs are glued into the counterbore recesses to cover the screw heads.

Directions: Nesting Office

MAKE THE DESK-LEG PAIRS. The legs for the desk base are made by joining desk legs (D) to ¾"-thick boards to form two leg pairs that will be fastened together with desk side boards to compete the base. The desk ends and desk sides form a frame, called the apron, that is used to support and fasten the desktop. Start by cutting the desk ends (B) and desk legs (D) to size. Sand all parts after cutting to remove any saw marks or splinters. Lay the legs on a flat surface, arranged in pairs, then lay the desk ends across the legs to form the leg pair assemblies. One desk end in each leg pair should be flush with the tops of the legs, and

Fasten the desktop to the desk base with brass corner braces.

the bottom of the other end board should be 10½" up from the bottoms of the legs. Clamp the leg pair assemblies together, then drill two pilot holes for #6 wood screws at each joint. Center the pilot holes over the joints, keeping them at least 1" away from the tops and bottoms of the end boards. Use a counterboring bit to counterbore these and all pilot holes in the project to accept ⅜"-dia. oak wood plugs. Unclamp the parts and apply wood glue to the mating surfaces, then fasten them to-

gether with #6 × 2" brass wood screws driven through the pilot holes. Double-check the assemblies with a square to make sure the legs are square to the end boards **(photo A).**

ASSEMBLE THE DESK BASE. Cut the desk sides (A) to length and sand smooth. Drill a pair of counterbored pilot holes about 1½" in from each end of each desk side board. Before drilling the pilot holes, check the leg pairs to make sure that the screws that are driven through the pilot holes will not run into the screws that hold the end

TIP

Always use brass or brass-plated fasteners when working with oak. Steel screws and wire brads will react with acid in the oak, causing the wood to turn black. Brass hardware, like hinges and corner braces, looks nice with oak, but if you install it after a protective finish is applied, the hardware doesn't need to be brass.

Install strips of oak cove molding between the underside of the desk-top and the desk apron. Miter the corners for a neater look.

TIP

Plain file boxes can be converted easily to hanging file boxes by installing a self-standing metal hanger system. Sold at office supply stores, the thin metal standards and support rods are custom-cut to fit the box, then assembled and set in place. The metal tabs on the hanging folders fit over the metal support rods.

boards to the legs. Adjust the pilot hole locations as needed. Apply glue to the mating end of one side board, and clamp it in place so it spans between the leg pairs, flush with the tops of the legs and desk ends. Check to make sure the leg pairs are square to the desk side, then drive #6 × 2" brass wood screws through the pilot holes. Install the other top side board the same way. Then, attach the lower side boards so the tops are flush with the tops of the end boards in the leg pairs. After the glue has set, apply glue to the ends of ⅜"-dia. oak wood plugs and insert them into all screw hole counterbores **(photo B).** When the glue has dried, sand the plugs so they are even with the surrounding wood, then sand the entire desk base with medium sandpaper to smooth out the surfaces and dull any sharp edges.

ATTACH THE DESKTOP. The plywood desktop is positioned on top of the base and fastened with corner braces. Using corner braces (without wood

glue) allows the desktop to move just enough so it will not cause the wood to split as it expands and contracts—plywood and solid oak will expand and contract at slightly different rates. Start by cutting the desk top (C) to size. Then, sand the edges so they are smooth and even. Wipe the edges clean, then cut strips of self-adhesive oak veneer edge tape to fit the edges. Use a household iron set at low to medium heat to press

the veneer onto the edges, creating edge surfaces that can accept wood stain. After the adhesive cools, trim off any excess edge tape with a sharp utility knife, then sand the veneer joints smooth with fine sandpaper. Place the desktop face-down on your worksurface, and center the desk base on the desktop. The desk top should overhang the base by ¾" on all sides. Clamp the base in place, and arrange 1¼" brass corner braces along the inside edges of the desk side and end boards. Use at least two braces on the sides and one at each end. Drill pilot holes at the guide holes in the braces, then drive #6 × ¾" brass wood

Attach the credenza ends and end rails to the legs with glue and counterbored wood screws.

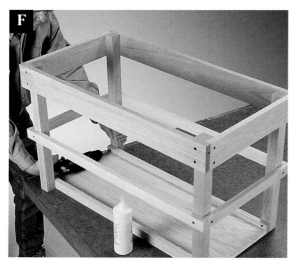

Fasten the bottom shelf by driving wood screws through the bottom rails and into the legs.

Cut notches at each corner of the middle shelf so it will fit around the credenza legs.

screws to attach the desktop **(photo C).**

ATTACH THE TOP MOLDING. The side molding (E) and end molding (F) fit underneath the desktop and are joined to the apron formed by the desk sides and ends. Cut the molding pieces to fit the desk dimensions. Miter-cut the ends of the side molding and end molding at a 45° angle. Position the side and end molding against the bottom of the desktop, and drill pilot holes in the molding for 1¼" brass brads. Apply glue to the backs of the side and end molding, including the mating surfaces of the mitered corners, and attach the molding pieces with wire brads **(photo D).**

MAKE THE CREDENZA BASE. The credenza base is built in much the same manner as the desk base. Leg pairs are formed, then joined by longer boards with wood screws and glue. Cut the credenza sides (G), credenza ends (H), middle rails (I), end rails (J) and credenza legs (K) to size. Arrange the legs in pairs with the end rails and credenza ends positioned across them.

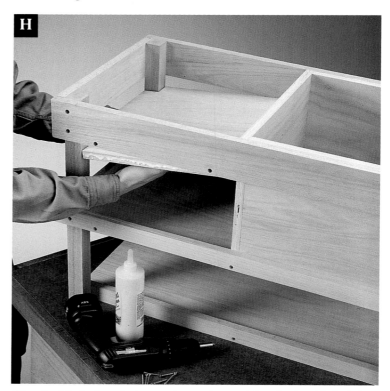

Glue the bin bottom between the credenza sides, flush with their bottom edges. Drive screws into the edges of the bin bottom to secure it.

The credenza ends should be flush with the outside edges and tops of the legs, and the end rails should be flush with the outside edges of the legs, with the tops of the rails 12" down from the tops of the legs. Clamp the parts together and drill counterbored pilot holes

for #6 screws at the joints. Disassemble, apply glue to the joints, then reassemble the leg pairs and drive #6 × 2" brass wood screws through the pilot holes **(photo E).** Stand the leg pairs on edge, and position the credenza sides and middle rails across them. Attach the side

I

Attach strips of oak stop molding to cover the exposed plywood edges of the bins on the outside of the credenza.

rails and middle rails to the leg pairs, the same way you attached the comparable parts when building the desk base.

MAKE THE CREDENZA SHELVES. Start by cutting the middle shelf (L), bottom shelf (M) and bottom rails (N) to size. Position a bottom rail against each long side of the bottom shelf. Make sure the ends are flush, and attach the bottom rails to the bottom shelf with glue and #6 × 2" brass wood screws, driven through the bottom rails and into the bottom shelf edges. Position the bottom shelf between the credenza legs so the bottoms are flush. Drive counterbored wood screws through the bottom rails and into the credenza legs **(photo F)**. Use a jig saw to cut 1½ × 1½" notches in each corner of the middle shelf, so it will fit around the credenza legs **(photo G)**. To attach the middle shelf between the middle rails and end rails, apply glue to the inside edges of the middle rails and end rails, and slide the shelf into position. The middle shelf should be flush with the bottom edges of the middle rails and end

rails. Use glue and screws driven through the middle and end rails to secure the middle shelf.

MAKE THE CREDENZA BINS. The credenza bins include a file box for hanging file folders, and a supply storage box. Both bins have flip-up lids. Begin by cutting the divider (O), end panel (P), side panels (Q) and bin bottom (R) to size. Cut 1½ × 1½" notches in both corners at one end of the bin bottom so it will fit around the legs. Position the side panels and end panels in place, and secure them by driving #6 × 1¼" wood screws through the side panels and end panels and into the rails and sides. Slide the divider into place so it butts against the side panels, forming a storage box in the upper section of the credenza. Fasten the divider with wood screws. On the opposite end of the credenza, drill evenly spaced pilot holes for the bin bottom in the credenza side and end, ⅜" up from the bottom edges of the boards. Apply glue to the edges of the bin bottom and position it in place, flush with the bottom edges of the credenza sides

and ends **(photo H).** Drive #6 × 2" wood screws through the sides and ends to secure the bin bottom. Cut the stops (S) to size from oak stop molding. Drill pilot holes, and use 1¼"-long brass brads to attach the stops to the centers of the joints between the panels, legs and divider **(photo I).** Cut the lids (T) to size from a single plywood panel. Use a household iron to apply oak veneer edge tape to the edges. Do not attach the lids until after the finish has been applied.

APPLY FINISHING TOUCHES. Insert oak wood plugs into any open counterbore holes in either the desk or the credenza, and sand smooth. Give both furnishings a final finish-sanding with 180- or 220-grit sandpaper, then apply your finish of choice (you may find it easier to finish the desk if you remove the desktop first—it is important that you finish the underside as well as the top). We used a clear topcoat only for a light, contemporary look, but you may prefer to use a light or medium wood stain first. When the finish has dried, reinstall the desk top. Fasten 3 × 1½" brass hinges to the bottom faces of the credenza lids, 2¼" in from the side edges. The backs of the hinge barrels should be flush with the back edges of the lids, when closed. Attach the lids to the credenza by fastening the hinges to the credenza ends. Attach sliding lid supports to the lids and credenza sides to hold the lids open while you reach in the bins. Finally, attach a 2½" swivel caster (brass housings will look best) to the bottom of each credenza leg.

Behind-the-sofa Bookcase

*This efficient bookcase fits right behind your sofa or up against a
wall to provide display space and a trimmed-out tabletop surface.*

CONSTRUCTION MATERIALS

Quantity	Lumber
2	1 × 10" × 8' aspen
1	1 × 8" × 8' aspen
3	1 × 4" × 8' aspen
2	1 × 2" × 8' aspen
2	1 × 3" × 8' chair rail molding

The space behind your sofa may not be the first area that comes to mind when you're searching for extra storage, but it does hold many possibilities for the space-starved home. This clever behind-the-sofa bookcase has display space below and a spacious tabletop that combine to make one slick wood project. The tabletop is high enough so it can be used as an auxiliary coffee table, if you don't mind reaching up for your beverage or snack.

We used aspen to build this table, then stained it for a natural appearance. If you prefer, you can build it from pine and paint it to match or complement your sofa.

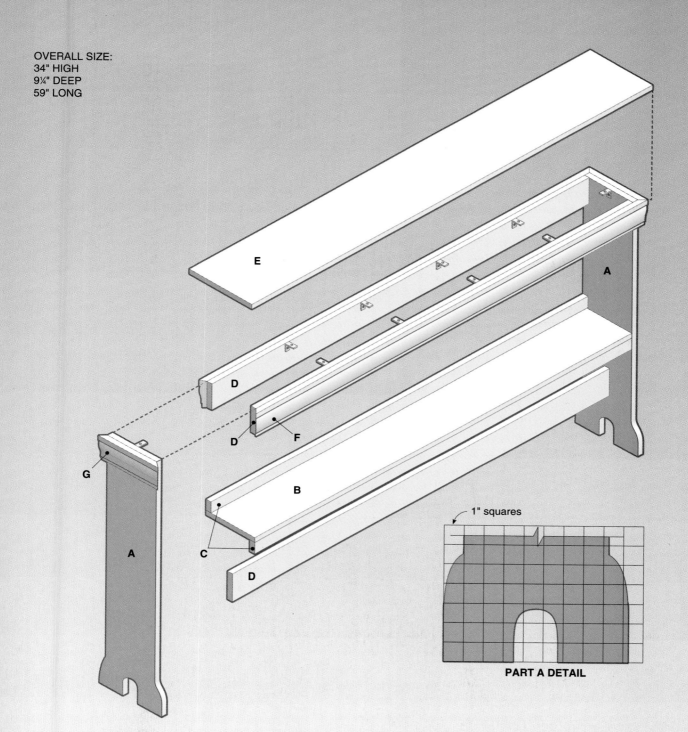

OVERALL SIZE:
34" HIGH
9¼" DEEP
59" LONG

1" squares

PART A DETAIL

Cutting List				
Key	Part	Dimension	Pcs.	Material
A	Leg	¾ × 9¼ × 33¼"	2	Aspen
B	Shelf	¾ × 7¼ × 55½"	1	Aspen
C	Shelf rail	¾ × 1½ × 55½"	2	Aspen
D	Stretcher	¾ × 3½ × 55½"	3	Aspen

Cutting List				
Key	Part	Dimension	Pcs.	Material
E	Tabletop	¾ × 9¼ × 59"	1	Aspen
F	Face trim	¾ × 2¼ × *"	2	Molding
G	End trim	¾ × 2¼ × *"	2	Molding

Materials: Wood glue, wood screws (#6 × 1¼", #6 × 2", #8 × ½"), 1¼" brass brads, 1½" corner braces (10), finishing materials.

Note: Measurements reflect the actual size of dimensional lumber.
*Cut to fit

Directions:
Behind-the-sofa Bookcase

MAKE THE LEGS. The legs for the bookcase are cut to shape with a jig saw. They feature decorative cutouts at the bottoms to add some style and to create feet that help with stabilization. Cut the legs (A) to the full size listed in the *Cutting List*, using 1 × 10 wood. Use the Part A Detail pattern on page 49 as a reference for laying out the cutting lines to form the feet at the bottoms of the legs. You may want to draw a 1"-square grid pattern at the bottom of one of the legs first. The safest way to make sure the shapes of the legs match is to cut one first, then use it as a template for tracing the shape for the second leg. Lay out the leg shape on one leg, using a straightedge to make sure the 1" relief cuts that run all the way up the edges of the legs are straight. Cut the straight section of one leg with a circular saw and a straightedge guide, and cut the patterned bottom with a jig saw. Sand the edges smooth, then trace the profile and cut the other leg **(photo A)**.

ATTACH THE SHELF & RAILS. The rails are attached to the front and back of the shelf to add strength and to create a lip in back so display items don't fall between the bookcase and the sofa. The front shelf rail fits

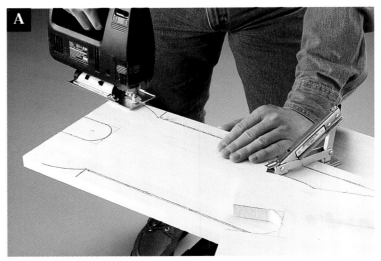

Draw the shapes for the legs onto pieces of 1 × 10, then cut with a jig saw. Make the long straight cuts with a circular saw.

Attach the shelf by driving wood screws through counterbored pilot holes in the legs.

up against the bottom of the shelf, flush with the front edge. The rear shelf rail fits on the top of the shelf, flush with the back edge. Cut the shelf (B) and shelf rails (C) to size, and sand the sharp edges slightly. Drill rows of pilot holes for #6 × 1¼" wood screws ⅜" in from the front and back edges of the shelf, for attaching the rails. Space the pilot holes at 8" intervals, then counterbore each pilot hole to accept a ⅜"-dia. wood plug. Make sure to drill the rows of counterbores on

opposite faces of the shelf from one another. Apply glue to the top edge of one rail, and clamp it to the shelf, making sure the front of the rail is flush with the edge of the shelf. Drive #6 × 1¼" wood screws through the counterbored pilot holes to secure the rail. Then, attach the other rail to the opposing face of the shelf. To attach the shelf and rails to the legs, first use a combination square to mark guidelines across one face of each leg, 16" up from the bottom. Drill pilot holes ⅜" down from

TIP

Crown molding is the molding type most frequently installed at the joints between walls and ceilings, but it also works well for trimming out the tops of cabinets, tables and other furnishings. Because it slopes downward when installed, making perfect joints can be a little tricky. Practice on some small scraps before you cut the actual trim pieces.

Use 1½" corner braces and ½" wood screws to attach the tabletop to the stretchers and the insides of the legs.

the guidelines, and counterbore the pilot holes. Apply glue to the ends of the shelf and rails, and position them between the legs so the top of the shelf is flush with the guidelines. Secure the shelf by driving #6 × 2" screws through the legs and into the shelf ends **(photo B).** Allow the glue to dry, and remove the clamps.

ATTACH THE STRETCHERS. Three stretchers fit between the legs at the bottom and top of the project to add strength and stability. A single lower stretcher is centered on the legs, while the top stretchers fit flush against the front and rear edges. The top stretchers anchor the tabletop. Begin by cutting the stretchers (D) to size. Before attaching the stretchers, carefully mark their positions on the inside faces of the legs. Center one stretcher 6" up from the bottoms of the legs, and attach it with glue and counterbored #6 × 2" wood screws, driven through the legs and into the stretcher ends. Attach the remaining two stretchers at the tops of the legs, flush with the front, top and back edges.

ATTACH THE TABLETOP. The tabletop is attached to the leg assembly with 1½" brass corner braces. Once the top is fastened, molding is cut to fit and attached to the top stretchers and legs, completing the sofa table. Start by cutting the tabletop (E) to size. Sand the top with medium-grit sandpaper to smooth out the edges. Turn the leg assembly upside down, and position it on the underside of the tabletop. Center the legs to create a 1" overhang at all sides. Clamp the legs to the tabletop, and use #8 × ½" wood screws and corner braces (four per side, one per end) to

secure the legs and stretchers to the tabletop **(photo C).**

INSTALL THE TRIM. The trim pieces that wrap the tabletop are cut from 3" crown molding, installed with mitered corner joints. Cut a piece of crown molding to about 64" in length to use for one face trim (F) piece, then place it against an edge of the tabletop and mark the ends of the tabletop onto the molding. Make 45° miter cuts away from the marks, then tack the piece in place with 4d finish nails. Cut the other long trim piece to the same size, and tack it in place. Use these pieces as references for cutting the end trim (G) pieces to fit. Remove the trim pieces, then refasten them with glue and 1¼"-long brads driven at regular intervals **(photo D).** Drive two brads through each joint to lock-nail the mating trim pieces together.

APPLY FINISHING TOUCHES. Glue ⅜"-dia. wood plugs into all couterbores, fill nail holes with wood putty and sand smooth. Finish-sand the bookcase with 180-or 220-grit sandpaper, then apply your selected finish. We used mahogany-tone wood stain and two coats of polyurethane.

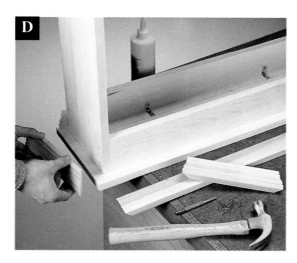

Wrap the edges of the tabletop with trim pieces made from 3" crown molding.

Computer Stand

Stack and protect your computer components to maximize desktop space, while providing dust protection and ventilation.

CONSTRUCTION MATERIALS

Quantity	Lumber
1	¾" × 2 × 4' birch plywood
1	1 × 4" × 8' pine/aspen
1	1 × 10" × 8' pine/aspen

It seems that no matter how big your desk is, there is never enough room for everything. One simple solution is this handcrafted computer stand. It's a stacking shelf unit that elevates your computer monitor to eye level to relieve neck strain, houses the processing unit in an accessible, well-ventilated location, and provides a handy tuck-under storage compartment for the keyboard when you're not using it.

If you own quite a few components, you can build as many computer stands as you need to house all of your equipment—they're stackable (but you probably will want to eliminate the keyboard door).

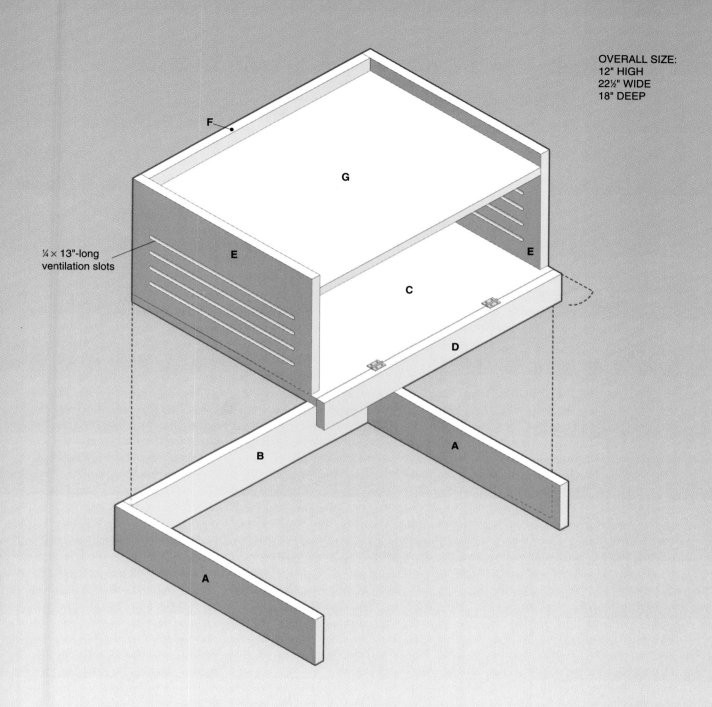

OVERALL SIZE:
12" HIGH
22½" WIDE
18" DEEP

¼ × 13"-long
ventilation slots

F

G

E   E

C

D

A

B

A

A

Cutting List

Key	Part	Dimension	Pcs.	Material
A	Base side	¾ × 3½ × 18"	2	Pine/aspen
B	Base back	¾ × 3½ × 21"	1	Pine/aspen
C	Lower shelf	¾ × 21 × 16½"	1	Plywood
D	Keyboard door	¾ × 2 × 20⅞"	1	Pine/aspen

Cutting List

Key	Part	Dimension	Pcs.	Material
E	Side	¾ × 9¼ × 16"	2	Pine/aspen
F	Back	¾ × 9¼ × 19½"	1	Pine/aspen
G	Upper shelf	¾ × 15¼ × 19½"	1	Plywood

Materials: #6 × 1½" wood screws, birch veneer edge tape, ⅜"-dia. wood plugs, wood glue, 1" butt hinges (2), finishing materials.

Note: Measurements reflect the actual thickness of dimensional lumber.

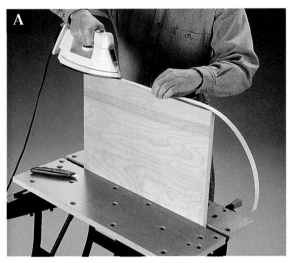

Apply self-adhesive veneer edge tape to the fronts of the shelves, using an iron to activate the adhesive.

Predrill counterbored pilot holes in the base frame before attaching the frame pieces to the lower shelf.

Directions: Computer Stand

MAKE THE BASE. The base section of this computer stand consists of a plywood shelf that rests on side and back strips. The base creates a low storage area designed to house a computer keyboard. If you plan to apply a natural wood finish to it, or if you want a very smooth painted finish, you should apply veneer edge tape to the front edge of the shelf at the top of the base (as well as the upper shelf). Cut the lower shelf (C) from ¾"-thick plywood (we used birch plywood), using a circular saw and straightedge cutting guide. Sand the edges and surfaces of the shelf with medium sandpaper to smooth out any saw blade marks and rough areas. Clean the edges thoroughly, then cut a strip of ¾" self-adhesive veneer tape slightly longer than the front edge of the shelf. Attach the tape by positioning it over the edge, then pressing it with a household iron set at a medium-low heat setting **(photo A).** The heat will

activate the adhesive. When the adhesive has cooled, trim the excess edge tape with a sharp utility knife. Sand the edges and surfaces of the taped edges with medium sandpaper to smooth out any rough spots. Cut the base sides (A) and base back (B) to length. You can use just about any wood for these parts. We used strips of aspen because it is a little harder than pine and it accepts finishing materials better. But pine, when given two or three coats of enamel paint, is a perfectly suitable option. Sand the edges and surfaces with medium sandpaper. Slip two ½"-thick scrap wood spacers beneath the lower shelf. Place the base back against the back edge of the shelf, keeping the ends and edges flush. Clamp the base back to the shelf and drill counterbored pilot holes for #6 × 1½" screws through the back and into the shelf, centered top-to-bottom on the shelf. Drill holes at 4" to 6" intervals. Remove the clamps and fasten the base to the shelf with glue and #6 × 1½" wood screws. Attach the base sides to

the ends of the base back and the side edges of the shelves, using glue and screws driven through counterbored pilot holes **(photo B).**

ATTACH THE KEYBOARD DOOR. The keyboard door is hinged to cover the open front of the base. When the computer is not in use, the door helps protect the keyboard while it is being stored in the base. The door is shorter than the base to make room at the bottom for the keyboard cords. Start by cutting the keyboard door (D) to length. Position a pair of 1 × 1" butt hinges on the top edge of the keyboard door, 4" in from each end. Mount the hinges to the door with the screws provided with the hinges. Then position the door between the base sides with the top edge flush with the top surface of the shelf. Mount the hinges to the shelf **(photo C).**

MAKE THE SIDES & BACK. The sides and back fit on top of the base to frame the storage area for the main computer processing unit. The parts feature ventilation slots to allow heat generated by the machinery to

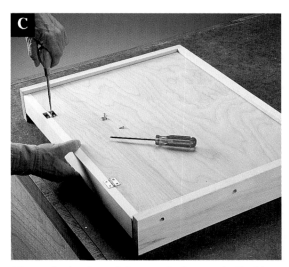

Mount the keyboard door to the lower shelf with butt hinges, then test for fit and operation.

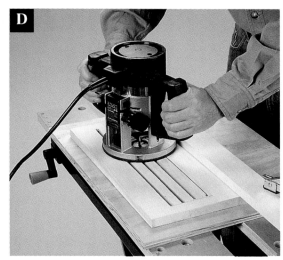

Cut ventilation slots in the sides and back with a router or jig saw and a straightedge cutting guide.

escape from the compartment. Start by cutting the sides (E) and back (F) to length from 1 × 10 wood. Next, lay out the ventilation slots in the sides and back with a combination square and pencil. Make the ventilation slots 13" long, stopping them 1½" from the end of each side and 3¼" from the ends of the back. Space the ventilation slots ¾" apart. The easiest tool to use to cut the slots is a router with a ¼" straight bit. If you don't own a router, you can use a jig saw with a thick blade to make slots, but because they will be narrower you should cut more of them. Whether you use a router or a jig saw, be sure to use a straightedge cutting guide. Clamp one of the side boards to your worksurface and position and clamp a straightedge cutting guide to align the router bit or jig saw blade with the ventilation slot to be cut. Drill ¼"-dia. starter holes at the ends of each ventilation slot (unless you are using a plunge router). Insert the router bit or jig saw blade into a starter hole and cut each slot

(photo D). If using a router, make multiple passes of increasing depth to avoid burning the wood. Usually ⅛" to ¼" depth per pass is adequate. Repeat the steps until all ventilation slots have been cut in both shelf sides and the shelf back. Sand the edges and surfaces of the boards.

FINISH THE ASSEMBLY. Cut the upper shelf (G) to size from ¾"-thick plywood and apply self-adhesive veneer edge tape to the front edge of the shelf, as you did for the lower shelf. Place the shelf upside down on ½"-thick spacers and position the back board (F) against the back edge of the shelf. Keep the ends of the back flush with the edges of the shelf. Clamp the parts together, drill counterbored pilot holes, then fasten the back to the shelf with glue and screws. Fasten the side boards (E) to the shelf and the back with glue and counterbored wood screws.

APPLY FINISHING TOUCHES. To allow access for power cords, you'll need to drill holes or cut slots in the back of the base and the back of the

processor storage area. For the neatest appearance, drill 1"-dia. holes at each end of the backs of these sections with a spade bit, then install a grommet in each hole (see *Tip,* below). One of the reasons for waiting until after the stand is assembled to make the holes or slots is so you can vary them according to the locations of the cords and ports on your components. After you've made the access holes or slots, insert glued ⅜"-dia. wood plugs into all the counterbores, then sand the plugs even with the wood surfaces after the glue has dried. Finish-sand all the wood surfaces. If you plan to apply a stain or a clear finish, do a final sanding with 180 or 220-grit sandpaper. Wipe down the entire stand with a rag dipped in mineral spirits, then apply your finish of choice. We used gray enamel paint to match the computer casings.

TIP

Install plastic grommets in the backs of furnishings that are designed to house corded equipment. Grommets are round inserts with cord holes that often are adjustable. They give most projects a more finished appearance.

Table/Chair

Based on a design from Colonial America, this clever furnishing features a tabletop that can be raised to form a backrest for a sturdy armchair.

PROJECT
POWER TOOLS

Living space was a valuable commodity in the tiny cottages of Colonial America. One clever solution they devised to solve the space crunch was the unique table/chair. With a tabletop that flipped up to do double duty as a backrest, the table/chair was a prime example of multifunctional design.

The updated version of the table/chair offered here has the same sturdy construction and multifunctional use as the original, although there are a few key differences you'll appreciate. Most notably, the tabletops of the majority of the original table/chairs were round. If your aim is to make as authentic a reproduction as possible, you can certainly build your own table/chair that way. But the difficulty of creating a perfectly round tabletop, together with the greatly increased wall space covered by the tabletop when raised, make the square version shown here an easier, less space-consuming project for most people. This table/chair design has the added

bonus of a generous storage compartment below the table shelf. And the fact that the broad surfaces in this furnishing are made from oak plywood makes it much easier to build than if you edge-glued pine boards together, as you likely would to make the original Colonial version.

CONSTRUCTION MATERIALS

Quantity	Lumber
1	1 × 6" × 8' oak
3	1 × 4" × 8' oak
1	¾" × 4 × 8' oak plywood
1	¾"-dia. × 12" oak dowel
1	⅜"-dia. × 12" oak dowel

OVERALL SIZE:
28⅝" HIGH
26⅛" WIDE
24" DEEP

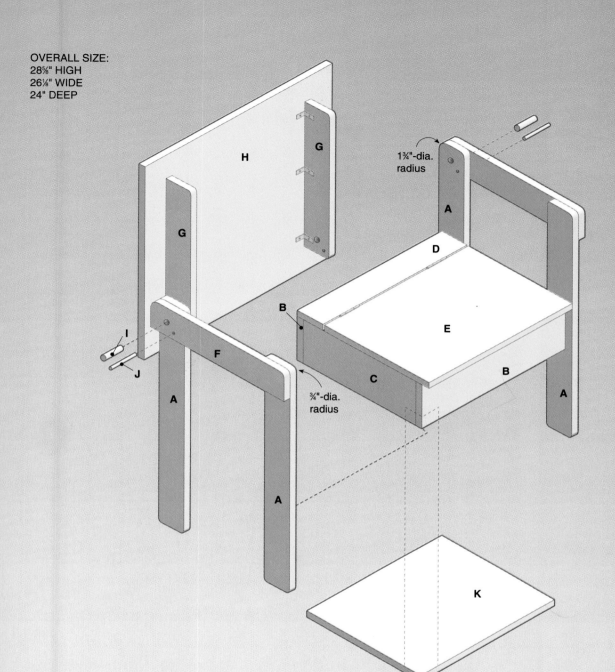

1¾"-dia. radius

¾"-dia. radius

Cutting List

Key	Part	Dimension	Pcs.	Material
A	Leg	¾ × 3½ × 28"	4	Oak
B	Box side	¾ × 5½ × 20"	2	Oak
C	Box end	¾ × 5½ × 15¾"	2	Oak
D	Hinge cleat	¾ × 3½ × 20"	1	Oak
E	Seat	¾ × 14½ × 19¾"	1	Plywood
F	Armrest	¾ × 3½ × 18"	2	Oak

Cutting List

Key	Part	Dimension	Pcs.	Material
G	Table cleat	¾ × 3½ × 18"	2	Oak
H	Tabletop	¾ × 24 × 26"	1	Plywood
I	Pivot	¾"-dia. × 2¼"	2	Oak dowel
J	Lock pin	⅜"-dia. × 3½"	2	Oak dowel
K	Box bottom	¾ × 15¾ × 18½"	1	Plywood

Materials: Wood glue, #6 wood screws (1", 1¼", 2"), 3 × 1½" brass hinges (2), brass corner braces (6), ¾" oak veneer edge tape (25'), 4d finish nails, finishing materials, paste wax.

Note: Measurements reflect the actual size of dimensional lumber.

The 1¾"-radius roundovers at the ends of the armrests and two of the legs allow the tabletop to pivot. Cut them with a jig saw.

Make sure the legs are square to the box frame, then fasten them together with glue and screws.

Directions: Table/chair

MAKE THE LEGS & ARMRESTS. The legs and armrests feature roundover cuts at the ends for increased stability and safety. Cut the legs (A) and armrests (F) to size from 1 × 4 oak. Use a compass to draw ¾"-radius curves on three corners of two of the legs, and at one end of the remaining two back legs. Cut the curves with a jig saw. On one corner of an armrest, draw a 1¾"-radius roundover and cut it with a jig saw. Use the roundover to trace identical curves at a corner of the other armrest, and at one square corner of the back legs. Cut the 1¾"-radius roundover in these parts **(photo A).** On the square end of each armrest, cut ¾"-radius curves on the corners.

BUILD THE BOX FRAME. Start by cutting the box sides (B), box ends (C) and box bottom (K) to size. Sand all parts with medium-grit sandpaper to smooth out any rough spots. Position the ends between the sides, then attach the sides and ends using glue and #6 × 1¼" wood screws, driven through the sides and into the ends. Be sure to drill evenly spaced pilot holes for the wood screws, counterbored to accept ⅜"-dia. wood plugs (throughout the project, counterbore all visible screw holes for ⅜"-dia. wood plugs). Next, use wood screws and glue to attach the bottom inside the ends and sides, flush with the bottom edges.

ATTACH THE BOX FRAME. The box frame fits between the legs, supporting the seat/shelf and creating storage. To attach it, first draw a reference line on one face of each leg, 10¾" up from the bottom. Clamp the armrests to the outside faces of the legs with the rounded corners up, keeping the top edges and ends flush. Make sure the 1¾" roundovers on the armrests

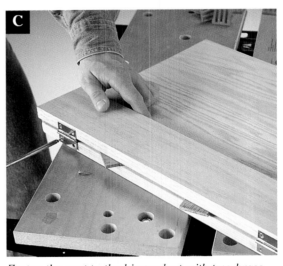

Fasten the seat to the hinge cleat with two brass butt hinges.

and the back legs are aligned. Position the box between the legs, so the top is flush with the reference lines on the legs. The box should be flush with the back edges of the rear legs, and ¾" in from the front edges of the front legs. Fasten the box between the legs with wood glue and #6 × 1¼" wood screws driven through counterbored pilot holes **(photo B).** Fasten the armrests to the outside faces of the legs with glue and #6 × 1" wood screws.

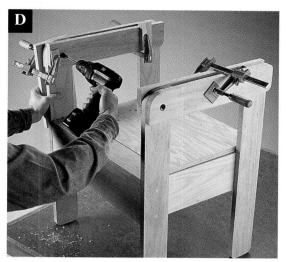

With a scrap block clamped to the outside of the legs, drill guide holes for the dowel pivots.

The tabletop is attached to the table cleats with brass corner brackets.

ATTACH THE SEAT. The seat (or shelf) for the table/chair is hinged to a 1 × 4 cleat that mounts to the back of the box frame. Start by cutting the hinge cleat (D) and the seat (E) to size. Cut strips of ¾" oak veneer edge tape to fit all four edges of the seat, then press them in place with a household iron. After the tape cools, trim off any excess with a sharp utility knife, then sand the edges smooth. Attach a pair of 3 × 1½" brass butt hinges to the mating edges of the hinge cleat and the seat board. Make sure any overhang is equal on each side. Install the hinges on the seat, about 2" in from each end, then fasten the seat to the hinge cleat **(photo C).** Attach the hinge cleat to the back edge of the box frame with glue and #6 × 2" wood screws.

MAKE THE TABLETOP. Start by cutting the tabletop (H) and table cleats (G) to size. Apply oak veneer edge tape to all four edges of the top. Use a compass to draw a ¾"-radius curve onto two of the corners of each cleat, aligned on the same edge. Cut the curves with a jig saw. Next, you'll need to drill guide holes for the dowel pivots. Clamp the table cleats to the inside faces of the legs, so the top and front edges are flush (also slip a scrap block over the outside face of each armrest before drilling). Mark drilling points that are 1¾" down from the top and 1¾" in from the back end of each armrest. Drill ¾"-dia. guide holes through the armrests, legs and table cleats at the drilling points, using a ¾" spade bit **(photo D).** Also mark drilling points for ⅜"-dia. guide holes for the lock pins ⅞" up from the bottom edges of the armrests and ⅞" in from the inside edges of the back legs. Drill the guide holes for the lock pins with a ⅜" spade bit. Cut the pivots (I) and lock pins (J) from oak doweling and test the fit.

APPLY THE FINISH. Before attaching the tabletop, apply a finish to the parts. We used medium-oak wood stain with two coats of polyurethane. Be sure to glue wood plugs into all counterbores and finish-sand thoroughly before applying the finish.

ATTACH THE TABLETOP. Replace the table cleats next to the legs and clamp in place with ⅛"-thick spacers between the table cleats and legs. Coat the pivot pins lightly with glue and drive them into the guide holes to join the table cleats, legs and armrests. Drill a pilot hole for a 4d finish nail through the back end of each armrest and into the pivot, then drive a finish nail to secure each pivot. Apply glue to the tops of table cleats, then center the tabletop over the cleats so it overhangs the legs by 3" at the front and back, and 1½" at the sides. Clamp the tabletop to the armrests, then fasten a 1¼ × 1¼" brass corner brace at each joint, about 1" in from the front of each table cleat. Unclamp the tabletop, then carefully tilt it up so you have access to attach the rest of the corner braces. Attach two more braces, evenly spaced, to the table cleats and the tabletop **(photo E).** Lower the tabletop, apply paste wax to the locking pins, then drive the pins into their guide holes to secure the top in the down position.

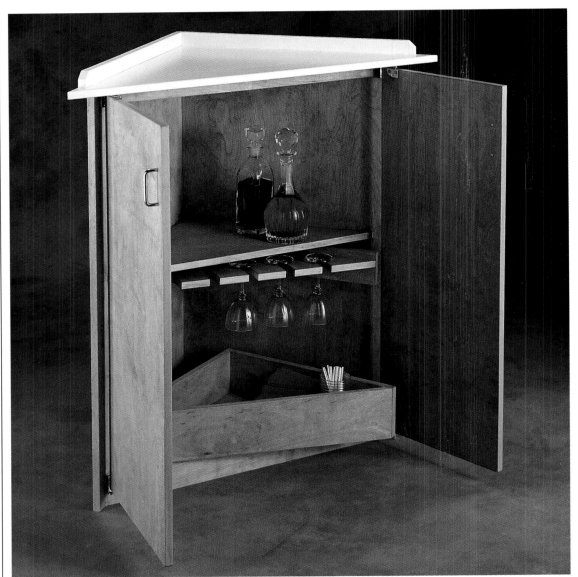

Corner Bar

*Slide the corner bar into an unobtrusive corner of your basement
or den to create a low-profile liquor cabinet.*

CONSTRUCTION MATERIALS

Quantity	Lumber
2	¾" × 4 × 8' birch plywood
1	¾" × 4 × 4' clad board
1	1 × 2" × 6' aspen
1	½ × ¾" × 4' shelf edge molding

This corner bar is perfect for a finished basement or study. It has plenty of room for all your wine and liquor bottles, plus a sturdy bin for mixed drink supplies and a convenient stemware rack for goblets and wine glasses. Both the bin and stemware rack are hinged on the inside of the corner bar to swing out for easy access.

The corner bar has plenty of room for supplies, but it doesn't call attention to itself. The triangular shape makes it easy to position in a corner of any room. The top is made with vinyl-clad particleboard for easy cleanup, and the storage bin and stemware rack are hinged so they swing out for easy access.

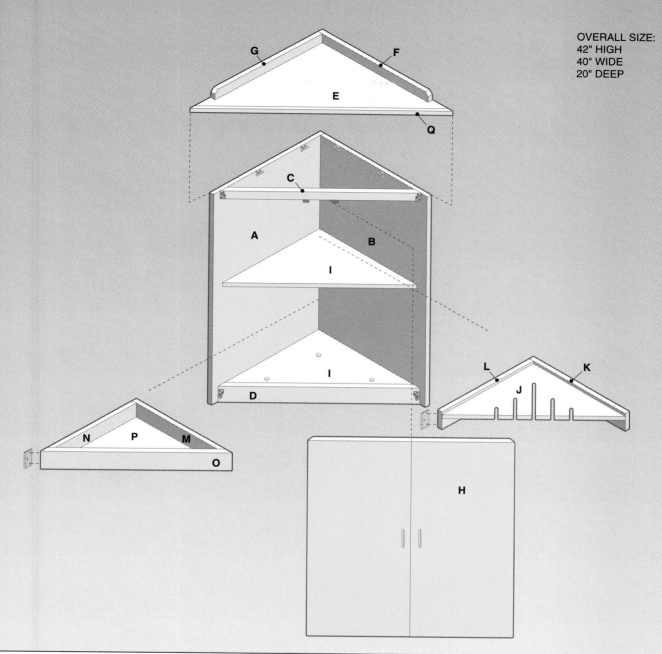

Cutting List

Key	Part	Dimension	Pcs.	Material
A	Long side	¾ × 24 × 41¼"	1	Plywood
B	Short side	¾ × 23¼ × 41¼"	1	Plywood
C	Top rail	¾ × 1½ × 31¼"	1	Plywood
D	Bottom rail	¾ × 3 × 31¼"	1	Plywood
E	Top	¾ × 28 × 28"	1	Clad board
F	Long splash	¾ × 1½ × 24"	1	Aspen
G	Short splash	¾ × 1½ × 23¼"	1	Aspen
H	Door	¾ × 16⅜ × 39"	2	Plywood
I	Shelf	¾ × 21⅛ × 21⅛"	2	Plywood

Cutting List

Key	Part	Dimension	Pcs.	Material
J	Stemware rack	¾ × 20 × 20"	1	Plywood
K	Long rack support	¾ × 3½ × 20"	1	Plywood
L	Short rack support	¾ × 3½ × 19¼"	1	Plywood
M	Long bin side	¾ × 5¼ × 20"	1	Plywood
N	Short bin side	¾ × 5¼ × 19¼"	1	Plywood
O	Bin front	¾ × 5¼ × 27"	1	Plywood
P	Bin bottom	¾ × 18⅛ × 18⅛"	1	Plywood
Q	Edge cap	½ × ¾ × 40"	1	Shelf edge

Materials: Wood glue, #6 wood screws (¾", 1½", 2", 2½"), 4d finish nails, small corner braces (6), 3 × 1½" zinc hinges (2), pin hinges (4), ⅞"-dia. domed nylon glides (3), wire pulls (2), finishing materials.

Note: Measurements reflect the actual size of dimensional lumber.

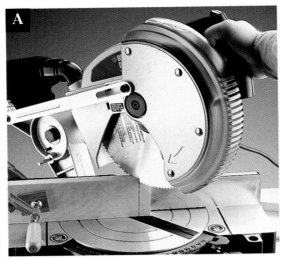

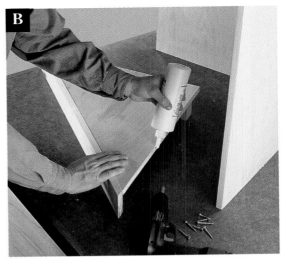

Use a miter saw to cut the top rail and bottom rail to fit between the cabinet sides.

Apply glue to the back of the bottom shelf and position it between the sides.

Directions: Corner Bar

MAKE THE CABINET SIDES. The cabinet sides form a "V" and fit flush with the walls in your room when the bar is positioned in a corner. Made from plywood, the exposed edges of the sides are covered with veneer edge tape so they can accept a clear finish (if you plan to paint the corner bar, you can simply fill the voids in the edges with putty, then sand them smooth). When the sides have been edge-taped and attached to each other at a right angle, rails are miter-cut and fastened between them on what will be the front of the bar. Start by cutting the long side (A) and short side (B) to size. Always sand parts after cutting to smooth out any rough spots and remove splinters. Use a household iron to apply adhesive-backed veneer edge tape to one long edge of the long and short sides—these edges will face the front of the unit. Fasten the long side to the short side with glue and #6 × 1½" wood screws, driven through the long side and into

Use the belt sander as a grinder to smooth out the edges of the top.

the short side edge. Make sure the top and bottom edges are flush. Countersink the holes so the screw heads will be recessed.

MAKE THE RAILS & SHELVES. The top rail and shelves are miter-cut to fit between the long side and short side. Cut the top rail (C) and bottom rail (D) to size. Use a power miter saw or miter box and backsaw to miter-cut the ends of the top

rail and bottom rail at 45° angles (photo A). Both ends should be cut facing in, allowing the rails to fit flush between the sides. Apply veneer edge tape to the bottom of the top rail and the top of the bottom rail. Cut the shelves (I) to size. The shelves are made easily by cutting a square piece of plywood in half along a diagonal line to form two triangles. Apply edge tape to the long edge of one shelf. Position the bottom rail against the long edge of the un-taped shelf. Make sure the top edges are flush, and attach the bottom rail to the shelf with #6 × 1½" wood screws, driven through the bottom rail and into the shelf. Counterbore the pilot holes to accept ⅜"-dia. wood plugs. Prop up the back corner of the shelf with a 2¼"-high piece of scrap wood, and push the bottom rail and shelf against the sides. Apply glue to the bottom rail and shelf **(photo B)**, and attach them between the sides with wood screws. (Drive #6 × 2" wood screws to secure the sides to the shelf, then drive a #6 × 1¼" wood screw through each side and into the bottom rail.) Position the top rail between the sides. Make sure the taped edge of the top rail is facing down and the top edges are flush with the top edges of the sides. Attach the top rail with glue and #6 × 1¼" screws, driven through the sides and into the ends of the top rail.

MAKE THE TOP. The triangular top is cut to size and fitted with a piece of shelf-edge molding along its front edge. We used clad particleboard to make the top. Clad board is a type of particleboard that is coated with vinyl or hard enamel to resist moisture. (Clad board is usually not suitable for painting.) If you are unable to find any of this material, you can either cut a piece of ⅛"-thick tile board and attach it to the top with panel adhesive, or simply use plywood and paint it with several coats of hard enamel paint. The top is attached with corner braces, which are installed on the sides and front rail. Start by cutting

the top (E) to the full size listed in the *Cutting List* on page 61. To cut the triangular shape, clamp a straightedge cutting guide to the square workpiece so the blade of your circular saw will cut just outside of a diagonal cutting line. Carefully make the cut, then clamp a belt sander to your worksurface, with the belt perpendicular, and use the belt sander like a grinder to even out any rough spots or saw marks **(photo C)**. Cut the edge cap (Q) from a piece of shelf-edge molding to fit on the front (long) edge of the top. Sand the edge cap to smooth out the edges, and paint it with several coats of enamel paint to match the top. Attach the edge cap to the top with glue and 4d finish nails driven through pilot holes **(photo D)**. Set the nails with a nail set, and fill the holes with wood putty. Touch up the holes with paint as needed. Drill pilot holes for #6 × 1¼" wood screws along the side

TIP

Be aware that one face of a piece of clad board will usually chip when you cut it. If you want both faces to be relatively free of chips, clamp a scrap piece of backer board to the top of the workpiece, and cut through the backer board and clad board simultaneously.

edges of the top. These pilot holes will be used when you attach the splash rails to the top. Attach two small corner braces on each side, and on the inside face of the top rail. Set the top in place so the sides are flush to the top edges, and attach the top to the corner braces with #6 × ¾" wood screws.

ATTACH THE SHELF. The remaining shelf fits between the sides, about halfway up from the bottom. Draw a line across the long and short sides, 22⅜" from the bottom. Drill pilot holes through the outside faces of the sides, spaced every 3" to 4", centered on the lines. Countersink the pilot holes enough

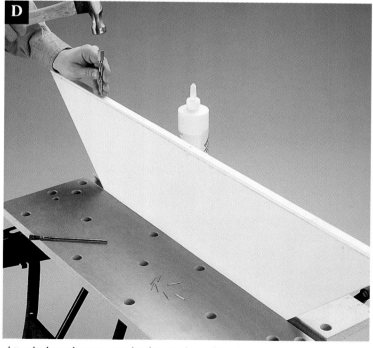

Attach the edge cap to the front edge of the top.

Attach the rack supports to the stemware rack with glue and screws.

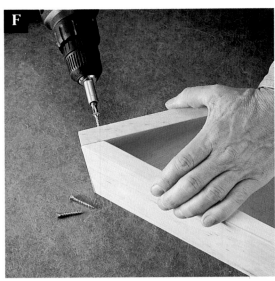

Drive countersunk wood screws through the bin sides and into the bin front.

so the screw heads will be recessed. Cut 3 pieces of 19"-long scrap wood to use as spacers when installing the shelf. Position the spacers inside the cabinet, and tape them against the inside faces of the sides. Apply glue to the nonveneer-taped edges of the shelf, and slide it into place on the spacers. Hold the shelf securely, and drive #6 × 1¼" wood screws through the sides and into the shelf edges.

MAKE THE STEMWARE RACK. The stemware rack is cut to size and notched to hold wine glasses, goblets and other types of stemware. Cut the stemware rack (J), long rack support (K) and short rack support (L) to size. Apply veneer edge tape to the front edge of the rack, and the top edges of the supports. The rack has evenly spaced, 1"-wide slots cut into it. We cut two 2½"-long slots, two 5"-long slots and one central 10"-long slot. Lay out the slots for stemware, starting on the front edge of the stemware rack, and cut the slots with a jig saw. Sand the rack and supports to

The bin rests on nylon glides and is hinged to the cabinet back.

smooth out any roughness. A round file is an excellent tool for smoothing out the slots. Or, if you prefer, cut the slots with a ½"-dia. straight router bit. Drill pilot holes through the long and short rack supports, 1⅛" down from the top (taped) edges. Apply glue to the side edges of the stemware rack, then fasten the rack between the long and short rack sup-

ports with wood screws **(photo E)**. It will help to position spacers beneath the stemware rack as you fasten it to the supports. Countersink the holes enough so the screw heads will be recessed.

MAKE THE BIN. The triangular bin is made to fit at the bottom of the corner bar. We also hinged the bin for access, but you may choose to fasten this

Mount the pin hinges to the beveled sides of the doors.

check for smooth operation. Mount another 3 × 3" hinge on one corner of the stemware rack, and attach it in the cabinet so the rack supports are 1" down from the shelf.

MAKE THE DOORS. Start by cutting the doors (H) to size. Bevel-cut one long side of each door with a circular saw set at a 45° cutting angle and a straight-edge cutting guide. When the doors are shut, the bevels will face inward, allowing the doors to swing wide instead of contacting the long and short sides. Edge-tape the three non-beveled edges of each door.

APPLY THE FINISH. Remove all hardware. Glue ⅜"-dia. wood plugs into all counterbores, and sand to level. Finish-sand all surfaces with 180- or 220-grit sandpaper. Apply your selected wood finish—we used a light penetrating wood stain with two coats of polyurethane. When the stain has dried, reinstall the hardware.

INSTALL THE BACKSPLASH. Cut the long splash (F) and short splash (G) to size. Attach the short splash to the long splash with glue and wood screws, forming a "V." Clamp the splash assembly to the top so the sides are flush. Drive #6 × 1¼" wood screws through the predrilled pilot holes in the top and into the bottom edges of the backsplash. Reinstall the top. Mount pin hinges to the top and bottom of each door along the bevel-cut edges **(photo H).** Attach the doors to the cabinet so the bottoms overhang the bottom rail by ½". Attach pulls and magnetic catches to the doors. The magnetic catches should fit on the top and bottom rails.

permanently as well if you prefer. Domed nylon glides are installed on the bottom shelf to prevent the bin from dragging across the bottom of the cabinet. Cut the long bin side (M), short bin side (N), bin front (O) and bin bottom (P) to size. Apply edge tape to the top edge of each piece, and use a power miter saw to miter-cut both ends of the bin front at a 45° angle. The miter cuts on the bin front should face in, allowing the bin front to fit flush against the long and short bin sides. Use glue and wood screws to fasten the short bin side to a side edge of the bin bottom. Make sure the short bin side is flush with the rear and bottom edges of the bin bottom. Fasten the long bin side to the bin bottom and short bin side. Attach the bin front to the bin bottom with

glue and wood screws. Counterbore the pilot holes for wood plugs. Fasten the ends of the bin front to the bin sides by driving countersunk, #6 × 1¼" wood screws through the bin sides and into the bin front **(photo F).** Center the screws ⅝" in from the front of the bin sides to avoid tearing through the bin front.

INSTALL THE STEMWARE RACK & THE BIN. Drive three ⅝"-dia. nylon glides into the bottom of the cabinet, spaced evenly apart (see *Diagram,* page 61). Test-fit the bin on the glides to make sure it rests evenly **(photo G).** Attach a 3 × 3" hinge to one corner of the bin. With the hinge in the closed position, position the bin in the cabinet, and trace the hinge position where it contacts the side. Install the bin hinge and

PROJECT
POWER TOOLS

Coffee Cabinet

*Even the tiniest kitchen can become a studio for the
art of making coffee with this compact oak cabinet.*

CONSTRUCTION MATERIALS

Quantity	Lumber
1	¾" × 4' × 8' oak plywood
1	⁷⁄₁₆ × 1¼" × 6' oak stop molding
1	¾ × ¾" × 6' oak cove molding

Making coffee has evolved from a routine chore into a gourmet pursuit in recent years. Where once a can of coffee and a percolator were the only tools you needed for your morning brew, today's arsenal of appliances and accessories has grown to include grinders, steamers, espresso makers, flavored additives, filters and much more.

It doesn't take many of these items to overrun a countertop.

We designed this coffee cabinet with today's more sophisticated coffee drinker in mind. The main compartment holds up to a 12-cup coffemaker, and the slide-out shelf and smaller storage compartments will handle filters, servers, grinders and just about any other coffee accessories you depend upon.

OVERALL SIZE:
15½" HIGH
22½" WIDE
13¼" DEEP

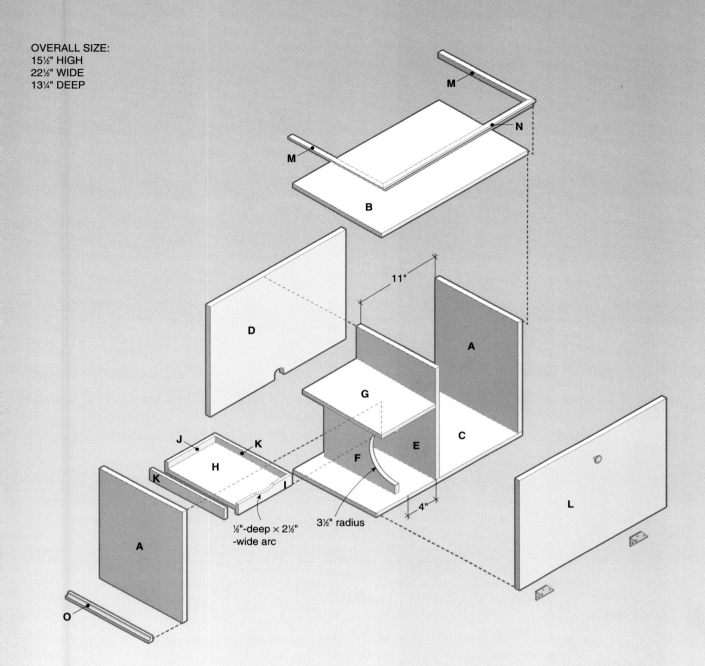

Cutting List

Key	Part	Dimension	Pcs.	Material
A	Side	¾ × 11¾ × 14"	2	Oak plywood
B	Top	¾ × 12½ × 21"	1	Oak plywood
C	Bottom	¾ × 11¾ × 21"	1	Oak plywood
D	Back	¾ × 14 × 19½"	1	Oak plywood
E	Divider	¾ × 11 × 14"	1	Oak plywood
F	Support	¾ × 9 × 10"	1	Oak plywood
G	Shelf	¾ × 7¾ × 11"	1	Oak plywood
H	Drawer bottom	¾ × 6¾ × 10"	1	Oak plywood

Cutting List

Key	Part	Dimension	Pcs.	Material
I	Drawer front	⁷⁄₁₆ × 1¼ × 7½"	1	Stop molding
J	Drawer back	⁷⁄₁₆ × 1¼ × 6¾"	1	Stop molding
K	Drawer side	⁷⁄₁₆ × 1¼ × 10½"	2	Stop molding
L	Door	¾ × 13⅞ × 21"	1	Oak plywood
M	Top side trim	⅝ × ¾ × 13¼"	2	Cove molding
N	Front trim	⅝ × ¾ × 22½"	1	Cove molding
O	Bottom side trim	⅝ × ¾ × 11¾"	2	Cove molding

Materials: Wood glue, wood screws (#6 × 2"), 1½ × 1½" brass butt hinges (2), magnetic catch, ¾" brass knob, oak veneer edge tape (25'), ⅜"-dia. flat oak plugs, 1¼" wire brads, ⅜"-thick rubber feet (4), finishing materials.

Note: Measurements reflect the actual size of dimensional lumber.

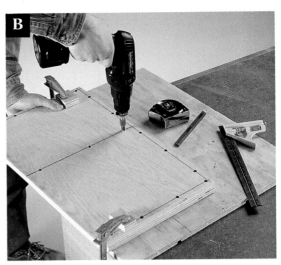

Using the support as a spacer, attach the shelf to the side, keeping the front and rear edges flush.

Clamp the top and bottom to your worksurface, and predrill pilot holes through both pieces.

Directions:
Coffee Cabinet

MAKE THE CABINET INSERTS. Cut the support (F) to size. A semicircular cutout is made in the front edge of the support to allow better access to the vertical storage slots. To make the cutout, find the midpoint of the front (short) edge of the support, measuring from top to bottom. Set the point of a compass at the midpoint, close to the edge. Draw a semicircle with a 2¼" radius on the support, centered from top to bottom on one short edge. Make the semicircular cutout with a jig saw. Next, cut the shelf (G) and sides (A). Sand all parts after cutting to smooth out any rough spots. Clamp the support against one of the sides, with the bottom edges flush. The support acts as a spacer for correctly positioning the shelf against the side. Butt a long edge of the shelf against the face of the side so the front and rear edges are flush. Make sure the bottom of the shelf is flush against the support. Attach the side to the edge of the shelf

with #6 × 2" wood screws, driven through pilot holes that are counterbored on the outside face of the side to accept ⅜"-dia. wood plugs **(photo A).** Unclamp the support, and mark a reference line on the bottom face of the shelf, 4" in from the free edge. Position the support on the bottom face of the shelf, flush against the reference line, and attach it with wood screws. Cut the divider (E). Position the divider against the free end of the shelf, making sure the front, bottom and rear edges are flush. Drive screws through the outside face of the divider and into the end of the shelf.

BUILD THE CABINET BOX. The top (B) and bottom (C) are attached to the shelf section and remaining side to form the cabinet box. Predrill all your counterbored pilot holes, following reference lines to ensure that the wood plugs you'll insert in the counterbores are aligned. Cut the top (B) and bottom (C). Position the top onto the bottom so the side edges and one long edge are flush, and clamp the parts to your worksurface. Mark refer-

ence lines on the top, ⅜" in from the side and rear edges. Drill evenly spaced, counterbored pilot holes for #6 × 2" wood screws along the side and back edges **(photo B).** Also drill pilot holes for the divider, 11⅜" in from the short side opposite the shelf section. Counterbore the screw holes on the top for ⅜"-dia. wood plugs. Unclamp the top and bottom. If you plan to apply a natural wood finish to the coffee cabinet (as we did), you'll need to cover the exposed edges of the plywood with strips of veneer tape. If you plan to paint the cabinet, you can skip this step, but make sure to fill in the voids and irregularities in the exposed edges with wood putty before you paint. Cut strips of self-adhesive veneer edge tape made from the same type of wood as the cabinet (oak, as shown). The strips should be slightly longer than the exposed edges. Make sure the edges are free of debris, then press the strips over the edges, using a household iron (the heat from the iron will activate

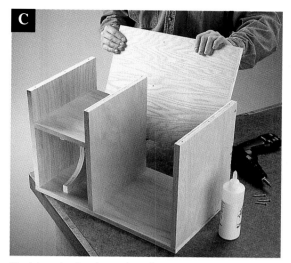

Position the back against the assembled frame, and attach it with glue and wood screws.

Lock-nail the mitered corners of the trim, and recess the brads with a nail set.

the adhesive). After the strips have cooled, trim off any excess at the edges with a sharp utility knife, then sand the edges smooth. Carefully position the shelf section onto the bottom. Make sure the side is flush with the front, rear and side edges of the bottom. Use glue and #6 × 2" wood screws to attach the shelf section. Position the free side at the opposite end of the bottom, flush with the bottom edges, and attach it. Cut the back (D). After you sand the back edges, position it against the rear of the cabinet frame **(photo C),** and attach it with glue and wood screws. Set the top onto the frame, and clamp it in place. Drive wood screws through the pilot holes to attach the top.

ATTACH THE TRIM. The trim is made from decorative cove molding. Cut the trim pieces (M, N, O) to length. Miter-cut one end of each top side piece and both ends of the front molding at a 45° angle so the pieces fit tightly together at the corners. Frame the front and sides around the top of the cabinet, and attach trim strips to the sides at the bottom of the

cabinet. To keep from splitting the trim, drill pilot holes before driving the 1¼" wire brads. Set all the brads with a nail set. Drive wire brads through the top corners where the front and side pieces meet, "lock-nailing" the joints **(photo D).**

MAKE THE DRAWER. The drawer is made by attaching oak stop molding to a plywood bottom. Cut the drawer bottom (H), drawer front (I), drawer back (J) and drawer sides (K). Mark a centered ¼"-deep × 2½"-wide arc on the top edge of the drawer, and cut the arc with a jig saw. Frame the drawer bottom with the front, back and side pieces, and attach with glue and wire brads **(photo E)**.

ATTACH THE DOOR. Cut the door (L) and apply veneer edge tape to the edges. Attach the door to the front of the cabinet with 1½ × 1½" brass butt hinges installed at the bottom edges of the door, starting 3" in from each end. Center the door on the front of the unit, and attach the hinges to the front edge of the cabinet bottom. Also install magnetic catch hardware at the top of the

Frame the drawer bottom with stop molding.

divider and on the inside face of the door.

APPLY FINISHING TOUCHES. Cut a 1 × 1½"-long notch in the back, centered on the bottom edge, so you can run appliance cords into the cabinet. Glue ⅜"-dia. wood plugs into all counterbores, and sand smooth. Finish-sand the cabinet with fine-grit sandpaper, then apply a finishing product (we used a warm oak penetrating stain). Topcoat the cabinet with two or three thin layers of water-based polyurethane. Attach ⅜"-thick rubber feet at each bottom corner, and attach a low-profile knob to the front face.

Corner Display Stand

This light and airy unit brings hardworking display shelving to any cramped corner of your house.

PROJECT
POWER TOOLS

The open back on this corner display stand lets you add a lot of display space to any room, without adding a lot of weight to the decor. Its roomy shelves are perfect for flower vases, fine china, souvenir-ware, picture frames and other knickknacks and collectibles.

CONSTRUCTION MATERIALS

Quantity	Lumber
7	1 × 4" × 8' pine
1	¾" × 4' × 8' plywood
1	¾ × ¾" × 6' cove molding

But this corner display stand is much more than a practical space-saver. The gentle arches on the front and the slatted back design blend into just about any decorating style. And because it's such a simple design, it doesn't draw attention away from the items on display.

This corner display stand is also very inexpensive to build. A single sheet of plywood is more than enough to make the triangular shelves, and the shelf rails and standards are made from 1 × 4 pine. The decorative trim pieces on the edges of the shelves are cut from ordinary ¾" cove molding. These materials, together with the painted finish, give the display stand a contemporary style. But if you're looking for furnishings with a more formal appearance, substitute oak boards and oak plywood, then apply a warm-toned wood stain.

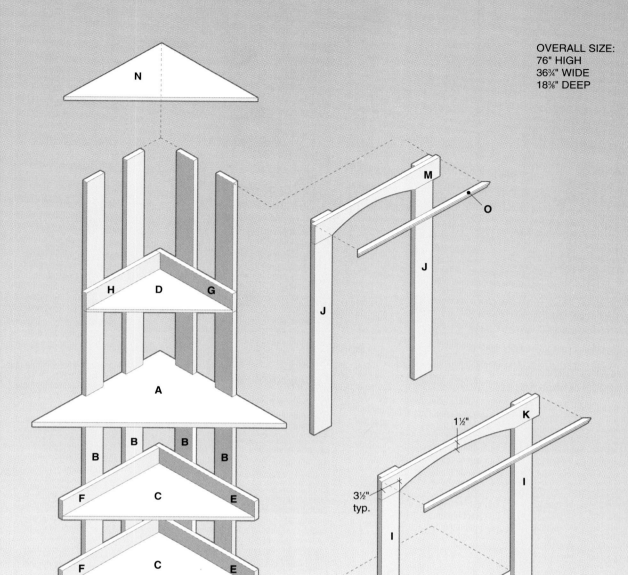

OVERALL SIZE:
76" HIGH
36¾" WIDE
18⅜" DEEP

1½"

3½"
typ.

Cutting List

Key	Part	Dimension	Pcs.	Material
A	Center shelf	¾ × 26 × 26"	1	Plywood
B	Standard	¾ × 3½ × 75¼"	4	Pine
C	Bottom shelf	¾ × 19½ × 19½"	2	Plywood
D	Top shelf	¾ × 15 × 15"	1	Plywood
E	Bottom rail	¾ × 3½ × 20¼"	2	Pine
F	Bottom rail	¾ × 3½ × 19½"	2	Pine
G	Top rail	¾ × 3½ × 15¾"	1	Pine
H	Top rail	¾ × 3½ × 15"	1	Pine

Cutting List

Key	Part	Dimension	Pcs.	Material
I	Lower stile	¾ × 3½ × 35¼"	2	Pine
J	Upper stile	¾ × 3½ × 39¼"	2	Pine
K	Lower front rail	¾ × 3½ × 32"	1	Pine
L	Lower front rail	¾ × 3½ × 30¼"	1	Pine
M	Upper front rail	¾ × 3½ × 25¼"	1	Pine
N	Top	¾ × 21¼ × 21¼"	1	Plywood
O	Trim	¾ × ¾ × 35"*	2	Cove molding

Materials: Wood glue, wood screws (#6 × 1½", #6 × 2"), 1¼" brads, finishing materials.
Note: Measurements reflect the actual size of dimensional lumber.   *Cut to fit.

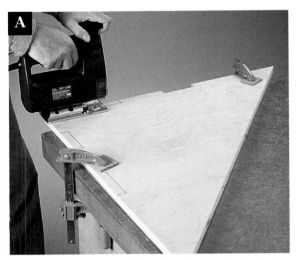

Use a jig saw to cut notches for the standards in the back edges of the center shelf.

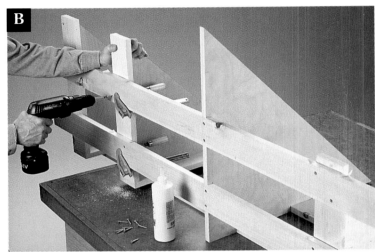

Drive screws through the standards and into the shelf rails.

Directions: Corner Display Stand

MAKE THE SHELVES. To make the center shelf (A), use a circular saw with a straightedge guide to cut a 26⅛" plywood square in half diagonally. The result is two triangles with 26"-long sides (the extra ⅛" allows for the thickness of the saw blade). Use a square to lay out ¾ × 3½"-long notches for the standards on the shelf sides, starting 4" and 12¼" in from each 90° corner, on each side. Cut the notches with a jig saw **(photo A).** Sand the shelf to remove any rough spots. To make the bottom shelves, cut a 19⅝"-square plywood piece in half diagonally. Cut the top shelf (D) to form a right triangle with two 15" sides. The top and bottom shelves are fitted with rails along the back edges. Cut the bottom rails (E, F) and the top rails (G, H) to length from 1 × 4 pine. Attach one longer rail (E) and one shorter rail (F) to the back edges of each bottom shelf so they make a butt joint and are flush with the ends of the shelf. Use glue and #6 × 2"

Use a flexible marking guide to draw the arches in the front rails.

Assemble the arched front rails and the stiles into face frames.

wood screws. Countersink all the screw pilot holes. Attach a longer top rail (G) and shorter top rail (H) to the back edges of the top shelf, so the bottoms are flush.

ATTACH THE STANDARDS. Cut the standards (B) to length. Sand the legs, and clamp them together with their tops and bottoms flush. Draw reference lines across the standards 3½",

16", 35¼" and 52" from one end. Then, draw reference lines on the shelf rails, 3¼" and 11½" on each side of the corner to mark the positions of the inside edges of the standards. Clamp the shelves to the standards so the reference lines are aligned, then attach the standards to the shelves with glue and #6 × 2" wood screws, driven through pilot holes in the backs of the standards and into the shelves **(photo B).** Note that the center shelf should be installed so the notches fit over the standards.

BUILD THE FACE FRAMES. The face frames give a finished look to the front of the display stand. They consist of vertical boards, called stiles, and horizontal boards, called rails. The rails feature decorative arcs. Cut the lower stiles (I), upper stiles (J), lower front rails (K, L) and upper front rail (M) to length. An easy way to mark the top and bottom arches is to use a thin, flexible piece of metal, plastic or wood as a marking guide. Find the centerpoint of each rail, and mark a point 13" in from the center in both directions. Tack a 1¼" brad at these points, as close to a long edge as possible. Also tack a brad at the centerpoint of each workpiece, 2" up from the same long edge. Hook the marking guide over the middle brad, and flex each end of the guide to the marked points. Trace the curve on each rail **(photo C),** and cut the curves with a jig saw. Position the shorter of the two lower front rails (L) across the lower stiles, with the arc pointing down. The edge of the rail containing the arc should be flush with the ends of the stiles, and the rail should over-

hang the outside edges of each stile by ⅞" (see *Diagram,* page 71). This is the bottom of the face frame. Clamp the rail to the stiles. Then, clamp the longer of the lower front rails (K) to the tops of the stiles, with the straight edge flush with the tops. The ends of the rail should be flush with the edges of the stile. Attach the lower front rails to the lower stiles with four #6 × 1¼" screws driven at each joint **(photo D).** Attach the upper front rail to the tops of the upper stiles, so the top and side edges are flush.

ATTACH THE FACE FRAMES & TOP. With the stand upright, slip the lower face frame in position. The bottom rail should fit beneath the lowest shelf, and the top rail should fit beneath the center shelf. Center the face frame from side to side so the overhang is equal. Clamp the face frame to the stand, then attach it with #6 × 2" wood screws driven through the stiles and into the edges of the shelves, and also driven into the top of each rail through the shelf above it **(photo E).** Position the upper face frame so

the bottoms of the stiles rest on the center shelf, and the stiles overhang the ends of the top shelf by equal amounts. Tack the face frame in place by driving one #6 × 2" wood screw through each stile and into the front edge of the top shelf. Then, drive screws up through the underside of the center shelf and into the bottom ends of the stiles **(photo F).**

APPLY FINISHING TOUCHES. Cut the top (N) to size, and attach it to the tops of the standards and the top rail of the upper face frame with glue and screws. The back sides of the top should be flush with the outside faces of the standards. To make the trim pieces (O), cut strips of ¾" cove molding to fit along the front edges of the center shelf and top shelf, with the ends miter-cut to follow the line of each shelf. Attach the trim pieces with 1¼" brads driven into pilot holes. Set all nail heads, then cover the nail and screw heads with wood putty. Sand the corner display stand, and paint with primer and two coats of enamel paint.

Drive screws through the center shelf and into the face frame.

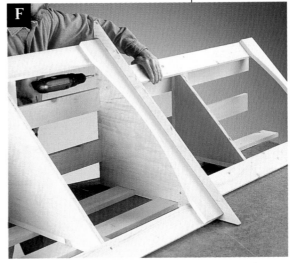

Drive wood screws up through the center shelf to secure the upper stiles.

PROJECT
POWER TOOLS

Folding Table

*Sturdy, spacious and portable, this indoor/outdoor
table folds up for storage.*

CONSTRUCTION MATERIALS

Quantity	Lumber
5	2 × 4" × 8' pine
6	1 × 6" × 8' pine
3	1 × 4" × 8' pine

Bigger and better than a card table, this efficient folding table can provide surplus seating at a moment's notice when company arrives. With more than 15 square feet of table surface, it is roomy enough for six adult diners. But when folded up for storage, it shrinks to a diminutive 3 × 3' package that is less than 12" thick—small enough to fit into just about any closet.

If you live in a house or apartment where outdoor security is an issue, this folding table can be stationed on your patio or balcony, then carted inside for times when you are not at home. If you plan to use the table outdoors, be sure to apply exterior-rated paint.

OVERALL SIZE:
29¼" HIGH
36" DEEP
63¼" LONG

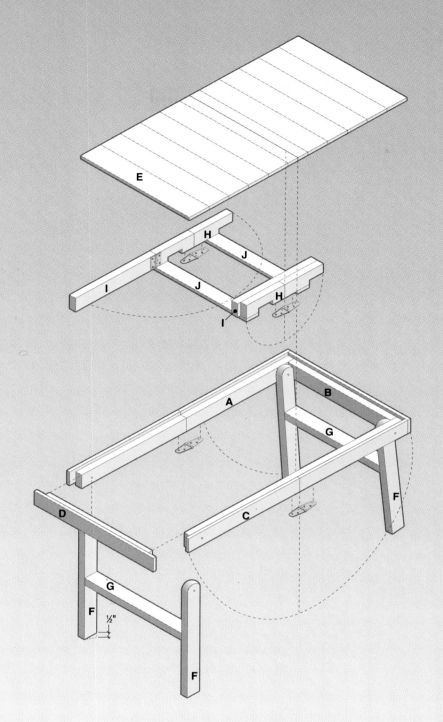

Key	Part	Dimension	Pcs.	Material
Cutting List				
A	Side rail	1½ × 3½ × 62"	2	Pine
B	End rail	1½ × 3½ × 31½"	2	Pine
C	Side skirt	¾ × 3½ × 63½"	2	Pine
D	End skirt	¾ × 3½ × 34½"	2	Pine
E	Slats	¾ × 5½ × 34½"	11	Pine

Key	Part	Dimension	Pcs.	Material
Cutting List				
F	Legs	1½ × 3½ × 28½"	4	Pine
G	Stretcher	1½ × 3½ × 28⅜"	2	Pine
H	Cleat	1½ × 3½ × 22"	2	Pine
I	Sweep	1½ × 3½ × 23"	2	Pine
J	Guide	¾ × 3½ × 28"	2	Pine

Materials: Wood glue, deck screws (1¼", 2", 2½"), 1½ × 6"-long strap hinges (4), 2 × 2" brass butt hinges (2), ⅜ × 4½" carriage bolts with lock nuts (4), 1"-dia. washers (8), finishing materials.

Note: Measurements reflect the actual size of dimensional lumber.

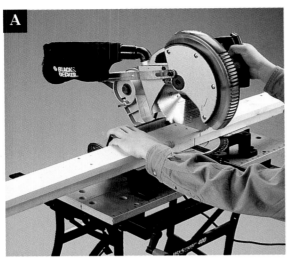

After attaching the side rails and side skirts, cross-cut them in half.

The middle slat is rip-cut in half and attached on each side of the hinged joint between the sides of the tabletop frame.

Attach the guides to the cleats, flush with the edges

Directions:
Folding Table

MAKE THE SIDE SECTIONS. Before permanently assembling the tabletop frame, the side sections are made. When fastening the parts, countersink all the screw holes. Start by cutting the side rails (A), end rails (B), side skirts (C) and end skirts (D) to size. Position a side skirt against each side rail. Make sure the side skirts overhang the side rails by ¾" on one long edge. This ¾"-wide overhang will face the top on the completed table, creating a lip for the slats (E) to sit on. Center the side skirts on the side rails so ¾" of the side skirts extends beyond the side rails at each end. Clamp the side skirts to the side rails, and attach the parts with 1¼" deck screws. Leave the middles of the side skirts and side rails free of screws so they can be cut in half. Once the side skirts and side rails are attached, draw reference lines across the center of the side skirts. Cut along the reference lines with a power miter box, cutting the boards into two equal lengths **(photo A).** Connect the halves with 6" brass strap hinges, attached to the bottom edges of the side rail halves. Unscrew the parts and hinges before proceeding.

ATTACH THE END SECTIONS. Like the side sections, the end sections are made with rails and skirts. Cut the end rails (B) and end skirts (D) to size. Position the end rails between the side rails, flush with the side rail ends. Apply glue, and drive 2½" deck screws through the side rail faces and into the end rails. Position an end skirt against each end rail. Like the relationship between the side rails and side skirts, there should be a ¾"-wide gap from the tops of the end skirts to the tops of the end rails. These gaps create a lip for the slats to sit on. With the ends of the end skirts flush with the side rails, drive 2½" deck screws through the end skirts and into the side rails and end rails. Reattach the side skirts with glue and wood screws, and reattach the strap hinges in their former positions.

ATTACH THE SLATS. Begin by cutting the slats (E) to size. Rip-cut one slat in half, using a circular saw and a straightedge guide. This halved slat will fit in the middle of the tabletop. Position one half of the ripped slat on each side of the cut at the center of the side rails. Butt the halved slat pieces together at the center so no gap is apparent. Attach each half to the side rails, using glue and 2" deck screws **(photo B).** Position the other slats across the tabletop frame, spaced evenly, and attach them with 2" deck screws.

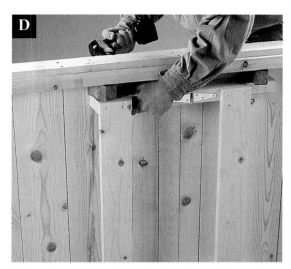

Drive deck screws through the slats and into the cleats below.

Fit the legs into place and attach them with carriage bolts, washers and lock nuts.

Drill ⅜"-dia. holes for carriage bolts through each end of the side skirts and side rails. Center the holes 4¼" in from the ends of the side skirts and 1¾" up from the bottoms of the side rails. The holes will be used to attach the legs.

MAKE THE LEGS. Cut the legs (F) and stretchers (G) to size. At one end of each leg, mark a point along one long edge, ½" in from the end. Draw a reference line from that point to the opposite corner on each leg. Cut along the reference lines with a circular saw. These slanted ends will be the bottoms of the legs. At the other end of each leg, use a compass to draw a centered, 1¾"-radius semicircle. Mark the center of the semicircle where the point of the compass was in contact with the workpiece. Drill a ⅜"-dia. hole for a carriage bolt through the centerpoint. Sand the legs smooth. Use a combination square to draw a reference line across one face of each leg, 14" down from the top. Position the legs in pairs on your worksurface. Slide a stretcher between each leg pair

with their top faces on the reference lines. Drill pilot holes, and attach the stretchers between the legs with glue and 2½" deck screws.

MAKE THE CLEATS. Start by cutting the cleats (H) to size. The cleats are notched on one long edge to allow the table to fold in half. Each notch is 1"deep × 3½"wide. To mark the notches, draw reference lines across one edge of each cleat, 3½", 7¼" and 18½" from one end. Use a pencil to shade from the 3½" line to the 7¼" line, and from the 18½" line to the ends of the cleats. These shaded areas mark the notches. Cut the notches with a jig saw, then cut each cleat in half. Attach the cleat halves with strap hinges, positioned across the centerline.

ATTACH THE SWEEPS & GUIDES. The sweeps (I) and guides (J) are attached to the cleats to form a locking mechanism. Cut the sweeps and guides to size. Position the guides on the cleats, flush with the edges of the notches. Attach the guides to the cleats with glue and 2" deck screws

(photo C). Turn the tabletop upside down, and position the cleats and guides inside the tabletop so their hinged centers align. Use 1¾"-thick spacers to center the cleats between the side rails. Trace the cleat outline onto the table slats with a pencil. Remove the cleats, and drill pilot holes through the slats in the tabletop. Insert the cleats and guides. Fasten them to the bottom of the table with glue and 2" deck screws **(photo D).** Make sure the center joints on the tabletop line up with the center joints on the cleats. Attach 3" brass butt hinges to one end of each sweep, then use the hinges to attach a sweep to one end of each cleat. Make sure the sweeps are attached at opposite ends of the cleats.

APPLY FINISHING TOUCHES. Fasten the legs inside the tabletop, using carriage bolts, washers and lock nuts **(photo E).** Check for smooth operation, then remove the hardware and fill all countersunk screw holes with wood putty. Sand the surfaces with medium sandpaper, and apply primer and paint.

Door-hung Ironing Center

Take advantage of the wasted space behind a door with this ironing center, which houses a board, iron and all your supplies.

PROJECT
POWER TOOLS

Even though we designed this ironing center for apartment living, it saves valuable floor space in any home. Liven up that dead space behind a door with this handy unit, which holds not only an ironing board, but also stores your iron and supplies. The low profile design allows the door to swing unimpaired, and because the ironing board is about two-thirds the size of a standard-size board, it folds neatly and cleanly into one attractive case. Just fold the board into the frame and close the ironing center door.

Hinged to a cabinet shelf in back and supported by a fold-down leg in front, the ironing center is very stable when mounted to the wall or door. With screws driven through the back pieces and into the door cross rails, you can even attach it to a hollow-core door.

It takes very little time or money to make this helpful project—if you've ever shopped for a wall-mounted ironing board, you know how expensive the prebuilt versions are. For people who are always scraping for more room in their home or apartment, the ironing center is a clever solution.

CONSTRUCTION MATERIALS

Quantity	Lumber
4	1 × 6" × 8' pine
1	1 × 4" × 10' pine
1	1 × 2" × 6' pine
1	¾" × 4' × 8' plywood

OVERALL SIZE:
60" HIGH
5½" DEEP
17" WIDE

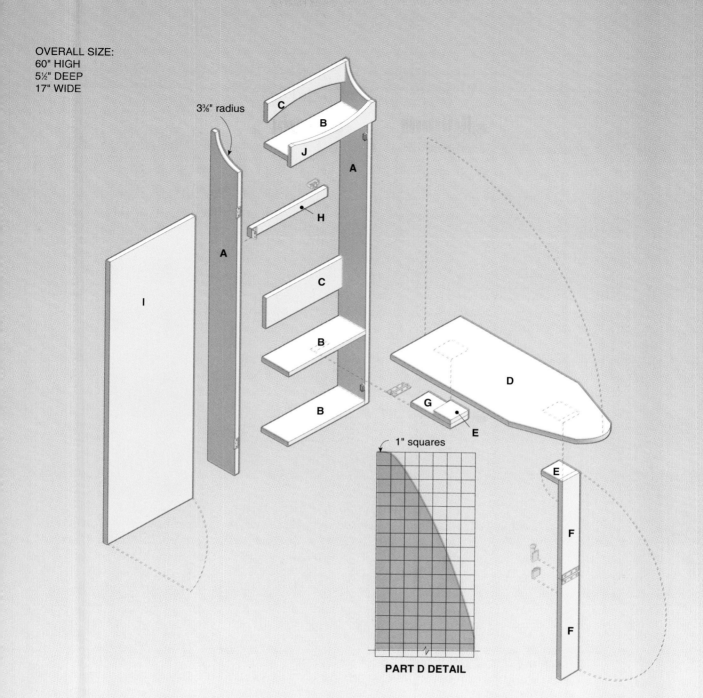

3⅜" radius

1" squares

PART D DETAIL

Key	Part	Dimension	Pcs.	Material
A	Side	¾ × 5½ × 60"	2	Pine
B	Shelf	¾ × 5½ × 15½"	3	Pine
C	Nailer	¾ × 3½ × 15½"	2	Pine
D	Ironing board	¾ × 14 × 36"	1	Plywood
E	Nailer block	¾ × 3½ × 3½"	2	Pine

Cutting List

Key	Part	Dimension	Pcs.	Material
F	Leg	¾ × 3½ × 18"	2	Pine
G	Support arm	¾ × 3½ × 8"	1	Pine
H	Hanger arm	¾ × 1½ × 15¼"	1	Pine
I	Door	¾ × 17 × 51¾"	1	Plywood
J	Top rail	¾ × 3½ × 17"	1	Pine

Cutting List

Materials: Wood glue, wood screws (#6 × 1¼", #6 × 2", #10 × 1½"), 3 × 1½" brass hinges (5), 2½" bolt catch, magnetic catches (2), roller catch (1), 2"-dia. wood knob, finishing materials.

Note: Measurements reflect the actual size of dimensional lumber.

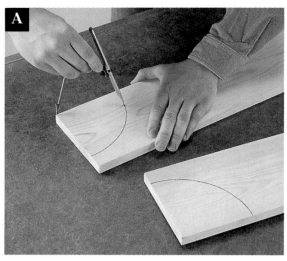

Use a compass to draw concave 4⅜"-dia. curves on the top, front corners of the sides.

Attach the top nailer between the sides, flush with their top sides.

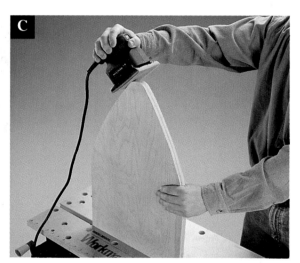

Use a power sander to smooth the edges of the ironing board after cutting it to shape.

Directions:
Door-hung Ironing Center

MAKE THE CABINET. Start by cutting the sides (A) and shelves (B) to length. Sand the parts to smooth out any rough spots. Position the sides on your worksurface, then use a compass to draw a concave 4⅜"-dia. curve at one end of each side **(photo A).** Set the point of the compass as close to each corner as you can when drawing the curve. Cut along the lines with a jig saw—these curved ends will be the

tops of the cabinet sides. Use a drum sander mounted in your electric drill to smooth out the curves. Cut the nailers (C) and top rail (J) to length. The top rail and one of the nailers each have a decorative arch cut on one long edge. An easy way to draw the arches is to use a thin, flexible piece of metal, plastic or wood as a marking guide. Mark points ¾" in from each end of the nailer and top rail on one long edge. Tack a 1¼" brad into these points, as close to the long edge as possible. Also tack a brad at the center of each workpiece, 1½" in from the same long edge. Hook the marking guide over the center nail, and flex each end to the marked points. Trace the arch with a pencil, and cut it out with a jig saw. Position the shelves between the sides. The bottom shelf should be flush with the bottoms of the sides. The middle and top shelves should be positioned so their bottom faces are 12¾" and 51¾" up from the bottoms of the sides. Drill countersunk pilot holes, and attach the shelves with glue and #6 × 2" wood

screws, driven through the sides and into the ends of the shelves. Attach the nailer without the arch cut on the edge between the sides, 5½" up from the top of the middle shelf, then fasten the arched nailer flush with the top and back of the sides **(photo B).** Make sure the nailer arch is facing down. Use glue and #6 × 2" wood screws to attach the top rail to the sides at the front edges. The arch should face the top of the ironing center, and the top edges of the top rail should be flush with the bottoms of the curves on the sides.

MAKE THE IRONING BOARD. The ironing board drops down and locks in place, supported by a leg and a swing-down support arm. Cut the ironing board (D) to size with a circular saw and a straightedge guide. Draw a 1"-square grid pattern on the ironing board, then draw the profile for the pointed front end, using the grid pattern from the *Diagram* on page 79 as a guide. Cut the ironing board shape with a jig saw, and sand the edges with a hand-held power sander **(photo C).** Cut

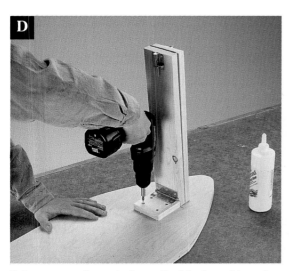

Drive screws through the nailer block and into the bottom of the board to attach the leg assembly.

Fasten the support arm and nailer block to the middle shelf with a brass butt hinge.

the legs (F), nailer blocks (E) and support arm (G) to size. Arrange the legs end to end on your worksurface. Keeping the joint between them tight, fasten a 3 × 1½" brass butt hinge to the legs (they fold together for storage in the cabinet). Turn the legs over and fasten a sliding bolt lock over the opposite side of the joint to lock the legs together. Position another butt hinge on one end of a leg, on the same side as the sliding bolt. Fasten this hinge so the barrel is ¾" in from the leg end. Set a nailer block on the leg with one end butting against the barrel of the hinge. Fasten the free end of the hinge to the nailer block. Apply glue to the nailer block, and attach it to the ironing board—the hinged edge of the block should be centered 7" in from the pointed end of the ironing board **(photo D).** Use glue and #6 × 1¼" wood screws to attach the remaining nailer block to the ironing board, centered 7" in from the square end. Using glue and wood screws, attach the support arm to the nailer block so the front edges and

side edges are flush. Fasten a butt hinge to the opposite end of the support arm.

INSTALL THE IRONING BOARD. Set the cabinet on your worksurface. Center the ironing board between the middle and top shelves. The legs should be facing up. Center the support arm and nailer block on the top edge of the ironing board, and attach the ironing board to the middle shelf, 1¼" in from the front edge of the shelf **(photo E).** Cut the hanger arm (H) to size. Attach a hinge to one end of the hanger arm, and the ball of a roller catch to the other end, on the opposite side. Mount the hanger arm inside the frame, 9" down from the top shelf. Mount the roller section of the roller catch, so the rollers are 1½" in from the front edge of the side **(photo F).**

HANG THE DOOR. Start by cutting the door (I) to size. Mount brass butt hinges on one long edge of the door. Attach a 2"-dia. knob to the outside of the door, 24" up from the bottom edge and 4" in from side edge. Install magnetic catches on the door and side.

APPLY FINISHING TOUCHES. Before painting the ironing center, you'll find it helpful to remove all the hardware. Fill any exposed screw holes with wood putty, and sand the surfaces smooth. Apply primer and enamel paint. Hang the cabinet on the door, about ½" down from the top edge (you can also hang it on the wall). Make sure the cabinet is level, and drive countersunk screws through each nailer, securing the ironing center to the door or wall. Reattach the hardware. Cover the board with a drawstring-type pad and cover.

Attach the roller catch to the unhinged end of the hanger arm.

PROJECT
POWER TOOLS

Exer-tainment Center

Combine your workout and entertainment space with this exercise
cabinet, which stores everything you need for morning workouts.

CONSTRUCTION MATERIALS

Quantity	Lumber
3	¾" × 4 × 8' plywood
1	¼" × 4 × 8' plywood
1	1 × 6" × 6' pine
6	½ × 1¼" × 6' stop molding

This modified entertainment center is designed for people who like to do their sit-ups, aerobics or stationary bike exercises in front of the TV. This "exer-tainment" center has room for a full-size TV and VCR, as well as shelving for sports equipment and video tapes. A fold-down, door-mounted bin for the stationary

biker keeps everything from a water bottle to a remote control in easy reach. We also attached a full-length mirror to the inside of the door, so you can monitor your form.

If you are not an active exerciser, eliminate the bins and tray, add shelves, and you'll have a simple entertainment center with traditional storage.

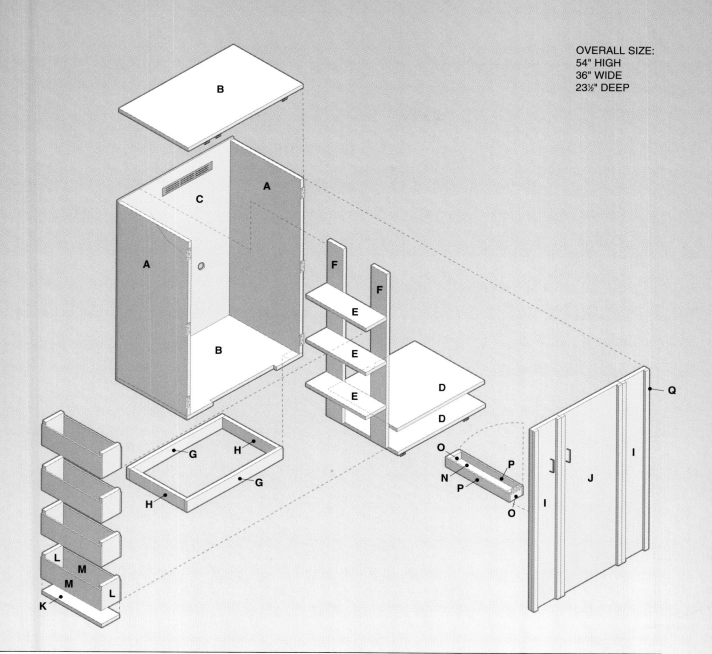

OVERALL SIZE:
54" HIGH
36" WIDE
23½" DEEP

Cutting List

Key	Part	Dimension	Pcs.	Material
A	Side	¾ × 22 × 49½"	2	Plywood
B	Top/bottom	¾ × 22 × 36"	2	Plywood
C	Back	¼ × 35¼ × 50¾"	1	Plywood
D	Large shelf	¾ × 21 × 27¼"	2	Plywood
E	Small shelf	¾ × 6¾ × 19"	3	Plywood
F	Divider	¾ × 5 × 49½"	2	Plywood
G	Base side	¾ × 3 × 30"	2	Plywood
H	Base end	¾ × 3 × 17½"	2	Plywood
I	End door	¾ × 7⅞ × 51"	2	Plywood

Cutting List

Key	Part	Dimension	Pcs.	Material
J	Middle door	¾ × 19¾ × 51"	1	Plywood
K	Tray bottom	¾ × 5½ × 17½"	4	Plywood
L	Tray end	¾ × 5½ × 6¾"	8	Pine
M	Tray side	¼ × 4¾ × 19"	8	Plywood
N	Bin bottom	¾ × 3½ × 18½"	1	Plywood
O	Bin end	¾ × 2½ × 3½"	2	Plywood
P	Bin side	¼ × 2½ × 20"	2	Plywood
Q	Door trim	½ × 1¼ × 51"	6	Stop molding

Materials: Wood glue, wood screws (#6 × 1½", #6 × 2"), 1¼" wire brads, 1" wire nails, 3 × 1½" brass butt hinges (10), brass door pulls (2), vent cover, tack-on nylon glides (16), finishing materials.

Note: Measurements reflect the actual size of dimensional lumber.

Directions:
Exer-tainment Center

MAKE THE DIVIDERS. Positioned on one end of the unit, the dividers hold the shelves firmly in place. Start by cutting the dividers (F) to size. Your first step is to drill pilot holes in the dividers. These pilot holes must be drilled carefully, since they will be used later as drilling guides for the cabinet sides (A). Begin by clamping the dividers together with their edges flush. Use a pencil and a combination square to mark reference lines across the dividers, 12⅛", 24⅝" and 37⅛" in from one end for the short shelves, and 14⅞" and 21⅝" in

for the long shelves. These reference lines mark the centers of the small shelves (E) and large shelves (D). Drill evenly spaced pilot holes on each reference line.

MAKE THE SIDES. Cut the sides (A) to size. Once the sides are cut, pilot holes are drilled through them for attaching the shelving. Draw a reference line down the length of each side, 3" in from one long edge. On one side, position a divider flush on the line, and set the other divider flush against the other long edge of the side. The divider pilot holes should align. Use a drill to extend the pilot holes through the dividers and into the side **(photo A).** Position the dividers in the same way on the other side panel. Since the short shelves are attached to just one side, you need only extend the long-shelf pilot holes into this side panel.

MAKE THE CABINET. Cut the top and bottom (B), large shelves (D) and small shelves (E) to size. Cut a 1"-deep × 21"-long notch on the front edge of the bottom, starting 7" in from the sides. Fasten the sides to the top and bottom with glue and #6 × 2" wood screws. Cut

the back (C) to size, and attach it to the cabinet with 1" wire nails, checking for square as you go. Use a drill with a 2"-dia. holesaw to cut holes in each long shelf **(photo B).** Position the holes at the center of each workpiece, 1" in from the rear edge. These cutouts let power cords pass through the shelves. Also use the drill and holesaw to cut an access opening in the cabinet back, 18¼" up from the bottom of the back. Also drill a starter hole in the back, and use a jig saw to cut a hole in the back for a vent cover (like the ones you use to cover soffit vents in your roof). The vent hole should be centered in the upper half of the cabinet back. Vent covers come in many sizes—make sure you measure your vent before cutting the hole. Paint the dividers, shelves and the interior of the cabinet.

INSTALL THE SHELVES. Position the cabinet on its back. Use the small shelves as spacers, and clamp the dividers in place. The front divider should be flush with the ends of the small shelves. The rear divider should be flush with the back. Attach the dividers with glue and wood screws **(photo C).**

Use the dividers as drilling guides when you drill the pilot holes for attaching the shelves and sides.

Drill power-cord access holes in the large shelves, using a drill fitted with a holesaw.

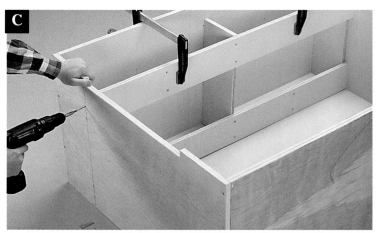

Attach the dividers by driving screws through the top and bottom and into the divider edges.

Outline the base on the bottom of the cabinet, then drill pilot holes for attaching the parts.

Sand the trays to smooth out any roughness and soften the edges.

The small shelves and large shelves fit flush against the back. Stand the cabinet upright. Use two 11¾"-long scrap boards as spacers to support the small shelves as you install them. Make sure the pilot holes in the side and dividers align with the small shelves, and attach the small shelves with wood screws. Install the large shelves on the opposite side of the dividers, using the pilot holes you drilled earlier in the sides and divider.

ATTACH THE BASE. The base fits under the bottom to support the cabinet. Cut the base sides (G) and base ends (H) to size. Fasten the base ends between the base sides. Countersink the holes to recess the screw heads. Position the cabinet on its back, and position the base onto the bottom. Trace the outline—there should be a 3"-wide gap between the front of the base and the unnotched front of the cabinet. Drill pilot holes **(photo D),** and attach the base with glue and #6 × 2" wood screws, driven through the bottom and into the base.

MAKE THE DOORS. Cut the end doors (I), middle door (J) and door trim (Q) to size. Use glue and wire brads to attach the trim pieces to each long edge of the end doors and middle door. Recess the brads with a nail set. Sand and paint the doors, then join one end door to the middle door to create a bifold-type door. Use two 3 × 1½" butt hinges at the joint. Set the doors aside.

MAKE THE TRAYS & BIN. Cut the tray bottoms (K), tray ends (L) and tray sides (M) to size. Use glue and #6 × 2" wood screws to attach the tray ends to the tray bottoms. Attach the tray sides to the tray bottom and ends with glue and 1¼" wire brads. Use a power sander to smooth out any rough spots on the trays **(photo E).** The bin is built in the same way as the trays. Cut the bin bottom (N), bin ends (O) and bin sides (P) to size. Fasten the bin ends to the bin bottom with glue and wood screws, then fasten the sides. Sand the bin smooth.

APPLY FINISHING TOUCHES. Fill screw and nail holes with wood putty. Finish-sand the unpainted parts of the project. Apply a primer and enamel or

Use a hinge to attach the fold-out bin to the left door, 28" up from the bottom of the door.

semi-gloss paint. Install a metal vent cover in the hole in the back. Fasten the bifold door assembly to the right side of the cabinet with butt hinges, and fasten the end door to the left side. Attach a butt hinge to one end of the bin, and fasten the other end of the hinge to the left door, 28" up from the bottom **(photo F).** Attach a roller catch to the inside of the unattached bin end and to the corresponding area on the door. Attach magnetic catches and pulls to the doors, top and one large shelf. Fasten a full-length dressing mirror to a door, and tack nylon glides to the bottoms of the trays.

PROJECT
POWER TOOLS

Pop-up Wine Bar

*Flip up the tabletop and slide out the oak plywood stools to enjoy a
a glass or two of your favorite wine vintage in an intimate setting.*

CONSTRUCTION MATERIALS

Quantity	Lumber
2	¾" × 4 × 8' oak plywood
1	2 × 2" × 4' oak
1	1 × 2" × 8' oak
1	¾ × ¾" × 4' oak quarter-round molding

S pecial wines deserve a
special environment to be
properly shared with a
friend. With this pop-up wine
bar, you can create an instant
cafe setting, complete with
stools and a wine rack. When
the wine bar is not in use, the
stools store neatly inside the
cabinet opening, and the bar
folds back down so the whole

unit is about the size of a small
bookcase. The storage rack at
the side is easily accessible at
all times, and the cabinet top
makes a handy surface for tem-
porary storage.

Made of edge-banded oak
plywood and solid oak trim
boards, the wine bar is a sturdy
piece of furniture that knows
how to conquer space.

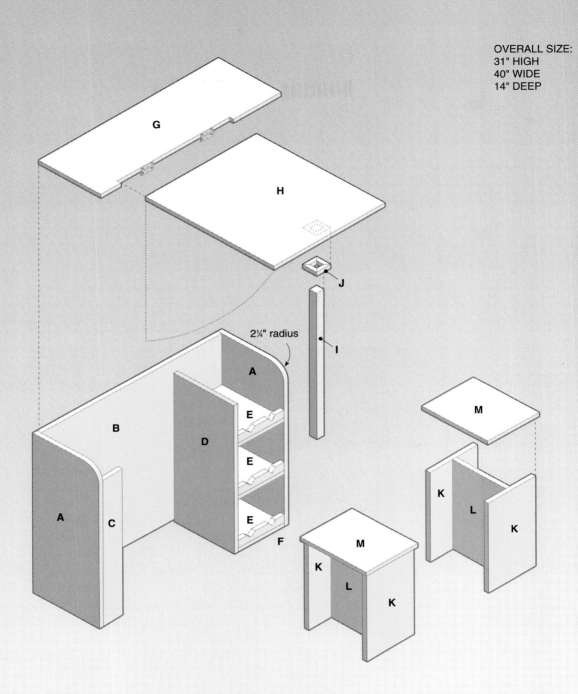

OVERALL SIZE:
31" HIGH
40" WIDE
14" DEEP

2¼" radius

Cutting List

Key	Part	Dimension	Pcs.	Material
A	Side panel	¾ × 14 × 31"	2	Oak Plywood
B	Back panel	¾ × 38½ × 31"	1	Oak Plywood
C	Filler strip	¾ × 4¼ × 28¼"	1	Oak Plywood
D	Center panel	¾ × 13 × 28¼"	1	Oak Plywood
E	Shelf	¾ × 9½ × 13"	3	Oak Plywood
F	Bottle support	¾ × 1½ × 8⅝"	3	Oak
G	Top panel	¾ × 13 × 38½"	1	Oak

Cutting List

Key	Part	Dimension	Pcs.	Material
H	Tabletop	¾ × 24 × 27"	1	Oak Plywood
I	Leg	1½ × 1½ × 28¼"	1	Oak
J	Leg molding	¾ × ¾ × 2"	4	Oak Molding
K	Stool side	¾ × 10 × 17¼"	4	Oak Plywood
L	Stool center	¾ × 11½ × 17¼"	2	Oak Plywood
M	Stool seat	¾ × 14 × 11"	2	Oak Plywood

Materials: Wood glue, #6 × 1⅝" wood screws, ⅜"-dia. oak plugs, finishing materials, 3d & 6d finish nails.

Note: Measurements reflect the actual thickness of dimensional lumber.

Cut the curves on the top front corners of the side panels with a jig saw.

Use a household iron to press veneer edge tape onto the plywood edges—the heat activates the self-adhesive backing.

Carefully trim off any excess veneer tape from the top and bottom, using a sharp utility knife.

Directions:
Pop-up Wine Bar

MAKE THE CABINET PANELS. The back and side cabinet panels form the main shell of the wine bar. We made them from ¾" oak plywood, with veneer edge tape to conceal the edges of the boards. The top, front edges of the side panels are rounded over, helping to create a three-sided splashboard that frames the tabletop. Cut the side panels (A) and back panel (B) to size, using a circular saw and straightedge cutting guide. Next, lay out the curved portions at the top front corners of the side panels with a compass set to form a curve with a 2¼" radius. Cut the curves with a jig saw **(photo A),** then sand the edges and surfaces of the panels with medium-grit sandpaper to smooth out any rough spots and saw marks. Clean the top of the back panel and the tops and sides of the side panels thoroughly, then cut strips of self-adhesive oak veneer edge tape to fit—use one strip only for each side to follow the curves. Place a strip over each edge, and set each strip in place by pressing it with a household iron set to low-to-medium heat **(photo B).** The heat activates the adhesive. When the adhesive has cooled and set, trim the edges of the strips with a sharp utility knife **(photo C),** then sand the edges and corners with medium-grit sandpaper to remove any irregularities. Clamp the side panels to the back panel so the sides cover the side edges of the back panel, and the bottoms

are flush. Drill pilot holes for #6 × 1⅝" wood screws at 6 to 8" intervals in the side panels, then counterbore the pilot holes for ⅜"-dia. wood plugs. Unclamp the parts, glue the edges and clamp them back together. Drive 1⅝" wood screws through the pilot holes to reinforce the joints.

INSTALL THE SHELF UNIT. The shelf unit fits on the right side of the cabinet to create storage space for six wine bottles. The shelves that support the wine bottles are spaced about 10" apart for accessibility. If your wine collection consists of more than a half-dozen bottles, you can easily refigure the shelf spacing and add another shelf. A center plywood panel supports the shelves on the left side. Cut the center panel (D) and the shelves (E) to size. Apply veneer edge tape to the front edges of all parts. Then, stand the side panels and back panel assembly upright and fasten the bottom shelf at the bottom of the corner created by the right side panel and the back panel. Use glue and wood screws driven through counter-

Rest the shelves on plywood spacers to make it easier for you to install the shelves, and to ensure that the spacing is accurate.

bored pilot holes. Next, fasten the center panel with glue and screws driven through the center panel and into the left edge of the bottom shelf. Also drive screws through the back panel and into the back edge of the center panel, making sure the distance between the center panel and the left side panel is the same at the top and bottom. To make sure the upper shelves are spaced correctly, cut two 8⅝"-long spacers from scrap plywood and place them on the bottom shelf. Set the middle shelf on top of the spacers so the front edge is flush with the fronts of the side and center panels. Fasten the shelf with glue and screws (make sure to counterbore all pilot holes). Then set the spacers on the middle shelf, and fasten the top shelf in place (photo D).

INSTALL THE BOTTLE SUPPORTS. The three shelves are trimmed in front with strips of 1 × 2 that feature pairs of V-shaped cutouts to support the necks of wine bottles. Cut the bottle supports (F) to length from 1 × 2 oak. Lay out the V-shaped cutouts for the bottle necks by measuring ¾" up from the bottom edge and 2½" in from each end and placing a mark. Using a combination square, mark a 45° angle in both directions from the marks to make the cutting lines for the cutouts (photo E). Cut out the V-shapes using a jig saw. Sand the edges smooth. Fasten the bottle supports to the tops of the shelves so they are flush with the front shelf edges. Use glue and 6d finish nails (drill pilot holes) driven through the shelves and into the bottoms of the supports. Also drive a nail though the side panel and center panel, and into each end of each support.

ATTACH THE FILLER STRIP & TOP PANEL. Cut the filler strip (C) and top panel (G) to size.

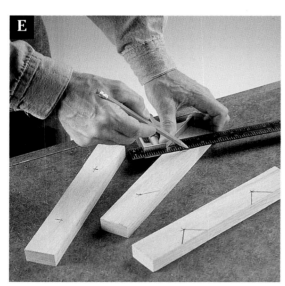

Use a combination square to lay out the V-shaped cutouts for the bottle necks.

The tabletop fits into a notch that is cut into the top panel with a jig saw—cut as straight as you can to make a clean joint.

The filler strip is installed on the left side of the cabinet to frame the cabinet opening and provide extra support for the tabletop. The top panel has a ¾" deep notch cut into the front edge to make a recess for hinging the tabletop. Lay out the notch on the top panel so it is ¾" deep, starting 10¼" from the right end and 4¼" from the left end. Cut the notch with a jig saw **(photo F),** using a straight-edge guide clamped to the board if you don't have a lot of experience cutting long lines with a jig saw. Smooth out the notch with medium-grit sandpaper. Apply veneer edge tape to the front edge and all three sides of the notch in the top panel, and apply tape to one of the long edges of the filler strip. Fasten the filler strip to the inside of the left cabinet side, flush with the bottom and ¾" back from the front edge. Use glue and #6 × 1⅝" wood screws driven through counterbored pilot holes. Then, install the top panel so it rests on the filler strip and the center panel, and the back edge is flush with the back panel (the front edge should also be flush with the fronts of the filler strip and the center panel). Use glue and counterbored screws, spaced at 8" intervals, to fasten the top panel.

MAKE THE TABLE-TOP. The tabletop is simply a rectangular piece of plywood with oak quarter-round molding fastened to the underside to hold the

TIP

When wine is stored, the bottles should slope down slightly toward the top. This ensures that the wine in the bottle stays in constant contact with the cork. Otherwise, the cork may dry and crack, allowing air, which can spoil the wine, into the bottle.

The top of the table leg fits into a square pocket created by pieces of quarter-round molding attached to the underside of the tabletop.

Invert the tabletop and side panel assembly and attach the butt hinges to the top panel, then fasten the tabletop to the hinges.

2 × 2 oak leg when the table is in use. Start by cutting the tabletop (H) to size from ¾"-thick oak plywood. Sand the edges and surfaces of the table top, then apply veneer edge tape to the edges of the tabletop. Sand the edges and surfaces smooth. Next, cut the leg (I) to length from 2 × 2 oak. Flip the tabletop upside down

and mark the leg pocket position by drawing a 1½" square that is 2" in from the front end and 11⅛" in from each side. Cut the leg molding (J) strips to frame the square and form a pocket to hold the leg. Miter the ends of the strips to make mitered joints at the corners of

Fasten the stool seat to the stool sides and stool centers with counterbored wood screws and glue.

the pocket (using a scrap of 2 × 2 as a gauge for the 1½" square will help quite a bit here). Fasten the molding around the square on the tabletop with glue and 3d finish nails **(photo G).** Test-fit the leg in the pocket to be assured of a proper fit.

INSTALL THE TABLETOP. Set the cabinet upside down on a flat worksurface. Then, set the tabletop upside down on two pieces of scrap 2 × 2 and position the tabletop against the notch in the top panel. Attach a pair of 2½" butt hinges to the front edge of the top panel, then fasten the hinges to the tabletop **(photo H).**

BUILD THE STOOLS. The simple, four-board stools are constructed easily from oak plywood panels. They are sized

to be housed for storage inside the opening in the cabinet part of the pop-up wine bar. Begin the stool construction by cutting the stool sides (K), stool centers (L) and stool seats (M) to size from ¾"-thick oak plywood. Apply wood veneer edge tape to the side edges of the stool sides and the perimeter edges of the stool seats. Trim the edge tape with a sharp utility knife and sand the edges and surfaces of the components with medium-grit sandpaper. Position the stool centers between the stool sides, centered on each stool side, then fasten the parts with counterbored #6 × 1⅝" wood screws and glue. Fasten the stool seat to the stool sides and stool centers with counterbored wood screws and glue **(photo I).**

APPLY FINISHING TOUCHES. Glue ⅜"-dia. oak wood plugs into all the screw hole counterbores, then sand the plugs flush with the surrounding wood. Drive the nail heads in the bottle supports below the surface, using a nail set. Sand all the wood surfaces and the edges of the wine table and stools with medium-grit sandpaper, then finish-sand the surfaces with fine-grit sandpaper. Wipe the wood clean with a rag dipped in mineral spirits, then apply a coat of sanding sealer and let it dry thoroughly. The sanding sealer helps the porous oak veneer layer absorb finish materials more evenly. Be sure to follow the manufacturer's directions and precautions when using any finishing material. After the sanding sealer has dried, using extra-fine sandpaper to lightly sand the sealed surfaces to remove any rough areas. Apply wood stain to the sealed surfaces with a paint brush or rag—a medium or darker-tone stain usually looks better with plywood than lighter stains. Let the stain dry completely, then apply two light coats of water-based polyurethane to the entire project. Add an extra coat or two to the surface of the tabletop.

TIP

Make sure the grain patterns run in the same direction when building with plywood. Even better-quality sheet goods, like oak plywood, tend to have very pronounced grain patterns, especially when you stain the wood. Having even one part in your project with grain running perpendicular to the other parts creates a very disappointing visual effect. Keep grain patterns in mind if you are making a sketch of how to cut the plywood sheets for most efficient use.

Gateleg Table

*Swing-out tabletop supports transform this wall-hugging oak
bistro table into a full-size dining table.*

CONSTRUCTION MATERIALS

Quantity	Lumber
6	1 × 4" × 8' oak
3	1 × 2" × 6' oak
1	¾" × 4 × 8' oak plywood

The gateleg table has become a standard furnishing in homes where space is tight. Typically, a gateleg table can be used as either a modest side table or, when fully extended, as a dinette-style table that seats four. This design thinks a little bigger. With the end leaves down, the tabletop measures 19 × 48" to provide plenty of space for two diners or for use as a bistro-style serving table. But when the end leaves are raised, this table expands to a spacious 67 × 48", giving you enough space for six diners with full table settings. And all this versatility is offered in a lovely oak package with fashionable slat-styling in the base.

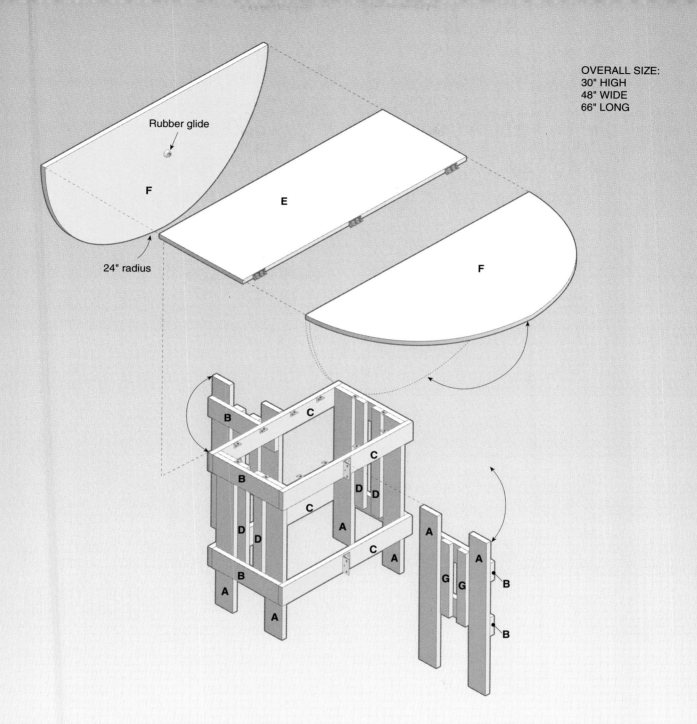

OVERALL SIZE:
30" HIGH
48" WIDE
66" LONG

Rubber glide

F

E

24" radius

F

B

C

B

C

C

D D

C

D

D

A

A

A

A

A

G G

B

B

B

B

A

A

A

Cutting List				
Key	Part	Dimension	Pcs.	Material
A	Leg	¾ × 3½ × 29¼"	8	Oak
B	Cross rail	¾ × 3½ × 14½"	8	Oak
C	Base rail	¾ × 3½ × 28"	4	Oak
D	Base slat	¾ × 1½ × 21"	4	Oak

Cutting List				
Key	Part	Dimension	Pcs.	Material
E	Table panel	¾ × 19 × 48"	1	Plywood
F	Table leaf	¾ × 24 × 48"	2	Plywood
G	Gate slat	¾ × 1½ × 14"	4	Oak

Materials: Wood glue, brass wood screws (#6 × 1¼", #6 × 2"), 1½ × 3" brass butt hinges (10), oak edge tape (25'), 1¼" brass corner braces (10), ⅞"-dia. rubber bumpers (2), finishing materials.

Note: Measurements reflect the actual size of dimensional lumber.

Attach cross rails to each pair of legs with glue and countersunk wood screws.

Position the base slats between the base legs, and attach them to the inside faces of the cross rails.

Directions:
Gateleg Table

BUILD THE LEG PAIRS. The support system for the gateleg table is made up of four pairs of 1 × 4 legs fastened to short 1 × 4 cross rails. Two of the pairs are connected with base rails to form the main table base. The swing-out gates each sport a single pair of legs. Start by cutting the legs (A) and cross rails (B) to size. Sand the parts with medium-grit sandpaper to remove any rough spots after cutting. Select four legs and four cross rails to build the leg pairs for the main base. Lay the legs flat on your worksurface, in pairs spaced about 7½" apart. Position a pair of cross rails to span across each leg pair. The ends of the cross rails should be flush with the outer edges of the legs, and the bottom of the lower cross rail should be 7¼" up from the bottoms of the legs. The upper cross rail should be flush with the tops of the legs. Use wood glue and #6 × 1¼" wood screws to attach the cross rails to each leg pair **(photo A).** Drill pilot

Sand the table base to smooth out any sharp corners or roughness.

holes for the screws, counterbored to accept a ⅜"-dia. wood plug, and check with a square to make sure the legs and braces are at right angles to one another before you permanently fasten them together. Next, assemble the leg pairs for the swing-out gates the same way, except for positioning the cross rails. The bottoms of the cross rails for the gates should be 14¾" and 25¼" up from the bottoms of the legs on these pairs.

INSTALL THE SLATS. Each leg pair features two decorative slats that are attached to the inside faces of the cross rails. Cut the 1 × 2 base slats (D) and gate slats (G) to length. Turn the base leg pairs over so the cross rails are facedown on your worksurface. Position two base slats on each leg pair so the tops of the slats are flush with the tops of the cross rails and the slats are spaced evenly, with a 1½"-wide gap between the outside edges of the slats

D

Mark the semicircular cutting line for the first table leaf with a bar compass (we made ours from a 25"-long piece of scrap wood).

TIP

Use very fine (400- to 600-grit) synthetic steel wool to buff your project between topcoats. This is especially helpful when using polyurethane, which is quite susceptible to air bubbles, even when very light coats are applied. Be sure to wipe the surface clean before applying the next coat.

and the inside edges of the legs. Use pieces of scrap 1 × 2 as spacers. Attach the slats to the cross rails with glue and #6 × 1¼" wood screws driven through counterbored pilot holes **(photo B).** Set the gate slats on the gates with the same spacing between slats, and the tops and bottoms of the slats flush with the tops and bottoms of the cross rails. Attach the gate slats to the gate cross rails with glue and screws.

ASSEMBLE THE TABLE BASE. The table base consists of the two pairs of base legs, connected by 1 × 4 side rails. Cut the base rails (C) to length, then drill a pair of counterbored pilot holes ⅜" in from both ends of each base rail. Prop the leg pairs in an upright position on a flat surface. Apply wood glue to the ends of the base cross rails, then clamp the side rails in position so the ends are flush with outer faces of the cross rails and the tops are aligned. Make sure all the joints are square, then drive #6 × 2" wood screws at each joint. After the glue in the joints has dried, apply glue to ⅜"-dia.

wood plugs and insert them into the counterbored screw holes. When the glue has dried, sand the plugs down so they are level with the surrounding wood. If the plugs are protruding more than ¹⁄₁₆" above the wood, use a belt sander with an 80- to 120-grit sanding belt to level off the plug, but be careful not to scuff up the faces of the rails **(photo C).**

MAKE THE TABLETOP. The tabletop top is made from three

pieces of plywood, trimmed with edge veneer tape. The rectangular table panel is mounted on the table base, and the end leaves are rounded, then attached to the table panel with butt hinges. Start by cutting the table panel (E) and table leaves (F) to the full measurements shown in the *Cutting List* on page 93. Use a bar compass to draw a centered, 24"-radius semicircle on one long edge of each leaf. If you don't own a bar compass, create a makeshift one from a 25"-long piece of straight scrap wood. Simply drill a ⅜"-dia. hole with a centerpoint ½" in from one end of the scrap to hold a pencil, then drive a 4d finish nail through a point ½" in from the other end. Attach the

E

Use an iron to apply oak veneer edge tape to all plywood edges.

Attach the table panel to the base with corner braces.

Attach the leaves to the table panel with 1½ × 3" brass butt hinges.

finish nail to a piece of plywood butted against one long edge of the leaf, insert the pencil into the hole, and draw the semicircle **(photo D).** Carefully cut the semicircle with a jig saw. To even out the cut, clamp a belt sander with a 120-grit belt to your worksurface so the belt is perpendicular to the surface and can spin unobstructed. Lay the table leaf flat on the worksurface (this is very important) and gently press the rounded edge of the leaf up against the spinning belt. Move the board back and forth across the belt until the edges are smooth and there are no irregularities in the semicircle. Use this table leaf as a template for tracing a matching semicircle onto the other leaf, then cut and shape the leaf the same way. Finally, press self-adhesive oak veneer edge tape onto all the edges of the table panel and the table leaves, using a household iron at low to medium heat setting **(photo E).** Trim off any excess tape with a sharp utility knife.

ASSEMBLE THE GATELEG TABLE. Before assembling the table parts, apply wood stain and a topcoat product (we used water-based polyurethane) to the parts, following the manufacturer's directions. After the finish has dried, position the top panel facedown on your worksurface. Center the table base on the underside of the top panel, and attach the parts with 1¼" brass corner braces **(photo F).** Next, butt the table leaves against the sides of the top panel, and fasten each leaf with two evenly spaced 1½ × 3" brass butt hinges **(photo G).** Attach a butt hinge to the outer face of each base rail, for attaching the gates. The hinges should be aligned, and positioned so the gate will be centered exactly on the rail. Attach a gate to each table side, making sure the tops of the gate and base are flush. Open the gates and extend them so they are perpendicular to the table base. Attach a ⅞"-dia. rubber glide to the underside of each leaf as a stop to keep the gate from swinging open too far **(photo H).**

Attach rubber glides to the tabletop to work as stops for the gates.